PROVERBS FROM MY FATHER

John Wilkerson

gracetogrow
PUBLICATIONS

PROVERBS FROM MY FATHER
© 2018 by Grace to Grow Publications
ISBN: 978-1-62289-002-6

All Scriptures used in this book are taken from the Holy Bible, King James Version, public domain.

ALSO AVAILABLE:
**Foundations
of My Faith Series**
*Bible studies designed
to help Christians grow in the
knowledge and love of Christ*

GRACE TO GROW PUBLICATIONS
507 State Street • Hammond, Indiana 46320
gracetogrowpublications.com • 219-629-8811

Printed and bound in the United States of America

DEDICATION

Richard Lynn Wilkerson
1937-1995

I CANNOT HELP BUT dedicate this volume to the man God used to have the greatest impact upon my life. He was a man who loved deeply, stood strongly, persevered passionately to train six children in the way they should go.

I pray that his insights and perspectives can provide helpful advice in our pursuit to do the same.

Pictured on adjacent page:
John Wilkerson with his mother,
Janelle (Wilkerson) Coleman

The Wilkerson family, July 1982
Front row, left to right: Matt, Dad, Mom with Tyler
Back row, left to right: Jeri Lynn, Luke, Mark, Janna, Mary.
John, and Linda

ACKNOWLEDGMENTS

G REAT GRATITUDE IS due to my mom, Janelle (Wilkerson) Coleman. She was our father's partner and completer. What a precious example of a godly wife and mother!

Thanks, Mom!

I would also like to commend and acknowledge the five others who called Richard Wilkerson Dad.

Matthew Wilkerson (Jeri Lynn)
Mark Wilkerson (Lori)
Janna Lee (Chris)
Luke Wilkerson (Jana)
Mary Mancia (Alex)

They each have enriching stories of growing up under the proverbs of our father. I love them and appreciate their role in my life and home while I was growing up.

TABLE OF CONTENTS

2. Teach children early to tithe and to give to faith promise missions.
3. Everyone should know that you are a Christian.
4. Be a Baptist by conviction.
5. Give your child a good name and help him to keep it good.
6. Remind your children that *Christian* means to be Christlike.

1. Keep your family in every church service and any other times the doors are open.
2. Don't allow children to play, run, write notes, eat, chew gum, or talk in church.
3. Don't let your children sit in church when they should be standing.
4. Wear the best you have to church to honor the Lord.
5. Keep your children in church and in the Word of God.

1. The Bible should be your child's most important Book.
2. Use the King James Version of the Bible.
3. Teach your children that Hell is real, creation is true, man's sinful nature is bad, and other basic Bible doctrines.
4. Teach them not to believe everything they hear or are taught but to test everything with the Bible.
5. Personally stay in the Word of God and in an attitude of prayer.

1. Teach your children to pray for and to help others.
2. Teach them to pray for others first and then themselves.

3. Pray for your children every time they come to your mind.
4. When taking a trip, ask the children to pray for safety.

Introduction
1. In family matters, speak to your children as adults
2. Children need a mother who will listen and love them.
3. Work diligently not to provoke your child to anger.
4. Listen to what your children have to say.
5. When you know the Lord's will on a matter, call the family together and tell them.
6. Endeavor to have family devotions regularly.

1. When disciplining your children, explain why you're disciplining them.
2. Don't spare the rod and spoil the child.
3. Don't let them play one authority against another.
4. Don't let your children make or take excuses.
5. Deal with children when they act like they are sinning or doing something that is wrong.
6. Never allow your child to talk back, throw a fit, or lie and get away with it.
7. Insist and see that your children do right.

1. Provide your children with a godly parent.
2. Show love and affection to your spouse in front of your children.
3. Don't allow them to ridicule the poor or handicapped.
4. Play with your children as much as you can.

5. Be careful to keep promises made to children unless providentially hindered.

1. Teach your children principles of friendship.
2. Train your children to be friendly to everyone.
3. Choose your children's friends.
4. Don't let your child visit overnight with a friend or a family that is worldly.
5. Teach your child not to be in the wrong place with the wrong crowd at the wrong time.

1. Help your children have the right kind of heroes— godly men and ladies.
2. Do not be talked into changing biblical convictions.
3. Don't let your children copy outlandish hairstyles or the fads of the world.
4. Make sure your boys get a good haircut, not a perm or a style.
5. Do not allow any rock music, country and Western, or contemporary Christian music.

Christian education is a must.

The Principle of Affection, Correction, Direction

Foreword

My Father, Richard Lynn Wilkerson

THE REASON I am a preacher of the gospel today is the result of a Sunday school teacher who had a burden for two little boys from Knoxville, Tennessee, in the late 1950s. That Sunday school teacher wanted more children in his Sunday school class. When he was knocking on doors, he found my dad and his little brother Douglas. He invited them to his Sunday school class. He eventually led my eleven-year-old dad to the Lord Jesus Christ one Sunday morning. The next week my dad's brother said, "I want him to talk to me too." The next week, Dad's brother accepted Jesus Christ. The two brothers became some of the first Christians in their family. My dad had no idea what it was like to be trained in a Christian home. Sadly, my dad was never discipled in the church he attended, so he grew very little in the Lord.

Unfortunately, my dad was reared in a home that did not know the Lord Jesus Christ. Chaos, dysfunction, and wickedness marked my dad's home life. Crystal balls, tarot cards, and foolishness of that nature was prevalent in his home. His mother was intoxicated regularly, and her addiction to alcohol would eventually result in her death due to cirrhosis of the liver. Thankfully, she came to know Christ as her Saviour before she passed away.

After graduating from high school, Dad joined the United

States Army and was stationed in Germany for part of his enlistment. At that time, he was away from the Lord and did not attend church. After serving his country, he returned to his hometown of Knoxville, Tennessee.

Coming home brought a change of heart in my father. His heavenly Father drew his wayward heart back to the things of God through salvation and the faithful love of a Sunday school teacher. To this day I am so thankful that my dad faithfully attended a Baptist church in Knoxville, Tennessee, where he was discipled and where he began to work in various capacities. Because Dad wanted to serve the Lord, he was eventually called to train for the ministry, so he enrolled in Bible college and graduated. There he met and married my mother, Janelle Benson, in 1966.

My parents' wedding day

Dad began pastoring a small country church when I was four years old, but he stepped away from the pastorate when I was six. He had served there nearly three years when he became overwhelmed with some of the responsibilities, the pressures, and the financial challenges. My father then began focusing much of his attention on training his six children for the Lord Jesus Christ. He did his best to rear them, to keep them in church, to teach them, and to love them. All of us have had the joy of knowing the Lord through salvation and loving the Lord through service.

Left to Right
ABOVE:
Dad (39)
Mom 35)
John (9)
Matt (8)

BELOW:
Mark (7)
Janna (5)
Luke (4)
Mary (1½)

The Wilkerson Clan 1976

Dad loved his kids, and he was very good about expressing his love. Nearly every day, Dad would speak to me and say, "I love you, John." I saw his love for me, my siblings, and the Lord.

Because of Dad's great love for God, he always kept his family in church. Even though we moved around like gypsies, Dad kept us in good Bible-believing churches. Now, with the Lord's help, four of his sons are in pastoral ministry. His oldest daughter is a missionary, and his youngest daughter has taught in a Christian school for over two decades. By God's grace, all of his grandchildren are in church. Words cannot express my thankfulness for this rich heritage.

The Bible says in Psalm 127:4, *"As arrows are in the hand of a mighty man; so are the children of the youth."* Arrows are not made to be stored in a quiver; they are made to be shot and to make an impact where the archer cannot go. My dad never preached on multiple continents, but his "arrows" have. My dad did not have the chance to win hundreds and thousands of people to Christ, but his arrows have. Dad can no longer tell people the wonderful message of salvation, but his arrows do.

We children had the joy of having Dad in our lives until February 1995 when he passed away from congestive heart failure and went to be in the presence of the Lord. We certainly miss him, but all of us are very thankful for the legacy of faith that he left us.

Dad was asked multiple times, "How did you raise such good kids? What did you do to turn out kids who want to serve the Lord?"

Dad would often answer that question in the same way by saying, "My kids have a really godly mother who listens to them…and a loud-mouthed father." Then he would always add, "And by the grace of God."

Obviously, Dad was not a perfect father; he did not do a perfect job, nor did he have perfect children. We children have

many areas in which to improve. Evidently though, Dad began thinking about that question he had heard multiple times because my mom found a notebook in which he had written some advice for parenting. He followed some principles that were very important for him to pass on. I believe these principles have been instrumental in my life, as well as in the lives of my five siblings. How grateful I am that Mom allowed me to see this notebook.

I believe these proverbs from my father are helpful to those who are rearing children. I also believe they are helpful to those of us who have left the childhood years. Quite frankly, the Bible will work for everyone because everyone needs the Lord's help. Some of the principles Dad taught are his strong opinions, but I do think all of them are substantiated by Scriptural principles. Certainly, I believe each of these lessons has the spirit of trying to help young people live for the Lord.

When my father went to heaven, he did not leave my siblings or me a monetary inheritance. He gave us something far greater than land, money, and possessions. He gave us a life that honored the Lord. He gave us principles that taught us how to live for the Lord. He gave us a love for the Word of God. He kept us in local, Bible-believing churches and taught us to be in church every Sunday for Sunday school, Sunday morning and Sunday evening services, and every Wednesday night. We were all beneficiaries of my dad's commitment to Christ, and I hope I can be just a portion of the dad to my children that he was to me.

From my dad's writings, I am pleased to give you his proverbs and principles of child rearing.

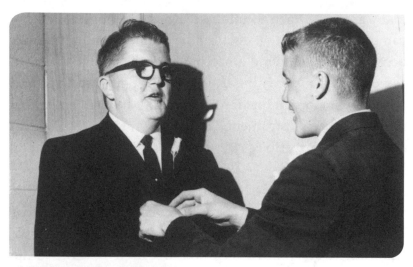

Above:
Richard Wilkerson with his
brother Doug

Left:
Richard and Janelle Wilkerson
with their firstborn son, John

Below:
Richard Wilkerson

BUILDING CHARACTER

A test of a Christian's character is what he does after he comes to the blockade in the road and what his attitude is after everything has left him except Jesus.

– Lester Roloff

INTRODUCTION

THE BIBLE OFFERS wisdom for parents who are rearing their children. Every parent should be seeking wisdom and grace to train those children under their care. I am certainly not a guru on the subject of child rearing. In fact, I am still in school, learning what God wants me to learn. I do not have all of the answers, but I did have a good father. My dad loved the Lord and was passionate about helping his kids do right. Because of his passion, he wasn't always easy to live with—especially when we were somewhat rebellious and not as compliant as we should have been. I'm very thankful for his affection, direction, and correction.

> Proverbs 7:1-3, *"My son, keep my words and lay up my commandments with thee. Keep my commandments, and live; and my law as the apple of thine eye. Bind them upon thy fingers, write them upon the table of thine heart."*

My father was fervent about the rearing of his children.

When I was four to six years old, Dad pastored a church in Picayune, Mississippi. As a pastor, he seemingly did a good job gathering about a hundred faithful people and constructing a church building. However, he became overwhelmed financially. Finances were not one of his strengths. As a result of that pressure, Dad never really found his fulfilling niche again in the Lord's work. However, he always remained faithful to church and made sure his family was in church. He turned his attention to helping six kids learn to love Jesus Christ and right. He was so intense about the matter that he would say, "The only thing I can take to heaven is my kids. I want to make sure my kids go to heaven." He exposed his kids to the Scriptures, to great churches, and to faithful pastors.

Our family moved frequently, and I often say my dad had "happy" feet. Even though we lived in many different cities, we always attended church and sat under the teaching of different pastors. My parents loved us so very much that they invested in us over and over again by taking us to revival meetings, camp meetings, and various conferences. We never missed a Wednesday night service or a Sunday service. If the church we were attending had an activity or special meeting, we would attend.

My parents paid a small fortune in school tuition, making sure we were in a Christian school. When I was in third grade, my dad learned about Christian education, so he took me out of the public school and enrolled me in a Christian school. I am eternally indebted to my dad for making this choice, but he didn't let the church or the Christian school rear his children. In every Christian school we attended, he'd say, "You should not be around certain kids in this school. I don't want you to be around so-and-so." My dad was the kind of man who thought he could pick my friends. He would hound me on choosing the right friends. As the oldest of six, obviously I took the brunt of the heaviness of my dad's discipline (though I am not sure my siblings would agree). I think he gave me a plethora of personal attention, and I'm very grateful. I surely wasn't overjoyed with his discipline at the time, but I am now very grateful for all that I learned from my dad.

Proverbs 7:1 says, *"My son, keep my words, and lay up my commandments with thee."* In this verse Solomon is saying,

"Know your father; listen to your dad." If you have a father in your life, you ought to listen to him. You should make his wish your command. Try to pay attention to what he does and who he is. Ask the Lord to help him. The Devil desires for fathers to be angry, abusive, addictive, aloof, or absent altogether. God's plan was to give children dads. Of course, Satan wants to remove fathers from the home and from their position of influence. I cannot stress the importance of fathers' taking that responsibility. The Bible does not say, "Mothers, provoke not your children to wrath but bring them up in the nurture and admonition of the Lord." God very plainly says, *"Fathers...."*

Obviously, we thank God for mothers. I am sure that Timothy thanked God for Lois and Eunice. I am sure that Jack Hyles thanked God for Coystal Hyles who reared that little boy with an absent father who was a drunkard. Thank God for many of our men and women who rear children alone. I have no greater admiration than for a lady or a man who rears children alone and walks alone with the Lord.

The following are a few of the principles that my father recorded in his book, though I did add the verses to the thoughts he had.

1.
TEACH YOUR BOYS TO WALK AND TALK LIKE MEN SHOULD.

TITUS 2:6 CONTAINS AN admonition to younger men: *"Young men likewise exhort to be sober minded."* This verse is saying to get serious. That verse doesn't mean that you cannot laugh or enjoy life. Young men need to realize their purpose. *"In all things shewing thyself a pattern of good works..."* (Titus 2:7). A *pattern* is "something that remains consistent."

I believe that one of the challenges of manhood for a young person is staying consistent. Young men of our society have been up and down like yo-yos. They're faithful for a little while, and then their faithfulness plummets. They read their Bibles for four or five days, and then they quit reading their Bibles. In the book of Titus, the young men were challenged to realize their purpose at this time of their lives. Ecclesiastes 12:1 says, *"Remember now thy Creator in the days of thy youth...."* This verse means "to remember your purpose, adopt a pattern of good works, and show consistency in the way in which you conduct yourself."

Titus 2:7 continues, *"In all things shewing thyself a pattern of good works: in doctrine* [what you believe and teach] *shewing uncorruptness, gravity, sincerity."* The word *gravity* means "down to earth," and *sincerity* means "genuine." As a rule, a young man usually struggles with controlling his mouth. In their youth, they tend to start cursing, losing their temper, and making ugly statements. The way for any person to have sound speech is to make sure his or her speech is what it should be.

My dad wanted my brothers and me to walk like men and talk like men. I was standing in line at a rental car agency when I couldn't help but notice a person standing nearby. The truth of the matter was, I didn't know if I was looking at a man or a woman. When the person finally turned around, I saw a beard, but I could not tell his gender by the way he walked or by the way he was dressed. Someone failed to teach that young man how to walk, how to talk, and how to conduct himself as a young man. I Corinthians 16:13 says, *"...quit you like men, be strong."* This passage addresses preparing oneself to be a man.

2.

TEACH YOUR GIRLS TO BE PROPER CHRISTIAN LADIES IN ATTITUDE, ACTIONS, AND ATTIRE.

TITUS 2:4, 5 SAYS, *"That they may teach the young women to be sober, to love their husbands, to love their children, ⁵To be discreet, chaste, keepers at home, good, obedient to their own husbands, that the word of God be not blasphemed."* *Sober* means "to realize their purpose." *Discreet* means "not out in front always seeking attention." The discreet woman is someone who is willing to help make a good thing better, easily adjusting to another's agenda. *Chaste* means "pure." Keepers at home learn how to perform the domestic tasks of life. *Good* means "generous."

A Christian young lady who is not a good example in these areas hurts the cause of Christ. The world should see a definite distinction. I am not sure why God doesn't give the same reference to the young men, but He does say that when a Christian young lady does not emulate those characteristics, she gives reason for the unsaved to blaspheme the Word of God. These verses have to do with her conduct, her attitude, and her attire.

Much of I Timothy 2 addresses the matter of prayer, but the focus changes in verse 9. *"In like manner also, that women adorn themselves in modest apparel, with shamefacedness and sobriety* [seriousness, down-to-earth, or with purpose]; *not with broided hair, or gold, or pearls, or costly array; But (which becometh women professing godliness) with good works."* In this passage, Timothy is giving instruction for ladies.

Ladies can choose to be frustrated by Timothy's instructions, which were given under the inspiration of the Holy Spirit, or they can say, "What does God want me to do?" I have discovered that ladies who find their role, play it, and exercise discretion, chastity, purity, submission, and teamwork with those who are in their lives are the happiest. These ladies find their fulfillment, and God brings them peace and joy because they are obeying the Word.

A principle given in Isaiah 47 speaks indirectly to women concerning their attitude about their attire. The Old Testament is given aforetime so believers can learn how God thinks. In this particular passage, God is chastising the children of Israel because of their behavior.

"Come down, and sit in the dust, O virgin daughter of Babylon, sit on the ground: there is no throne, O daughter of the Chaldeans: for thou shalt no more be called tender and delicate. Take the millstones, and grind meal [go into captivity]: *uncover thy locks* [let down your hair], *make bare the leg, uncover the thigh, pass over the rivers. Thy nakedness shall be uncovered, yea, thy shame shall be seen: I will take vengeance, and I will not meet thee as a man. As for our redeemer, the LORD of hosts is his name, the Holy One of Israel"* (Isaiah 47:1-4).

God is chastising this nation, especially their ladies. He is saying this rebellious people is no longer cherished because their chastity and discretion is missing. God tells them to go ahead and reveal the thigh. When girls or women wear clothing that reveals the thigh, they show what God calls *nakedness*. God says that the uncovered thigh is *nakedness*.

No wonder our world advocates that the shorter it gets, the better it is. Oftentimes, those who struggle in this area are the middle-aged ladies and teenagers. They seem to become more careless and not as sensitive to the Spirit of God in this matter. Some ladies may know exactly what they're doing, but some may not, but I can promise you that guys know exactly what the ladies are doing.

An entire chapter in Leviticus discusses God's feelings about nakedness. The only time nakedness is acceptable is when it is between a husband and his wife. The Bible says in Genesis 2 that the man and his wife were naked and not ashamed. I'm sorry to say that we live in a society where many ladies push the envelope on God's definition of nakedness.

Clothing is for four primary reasons:

1) **Dress is for protection.** Clothing protects from harmful effects of extremes in temperatures.

2) **Dress is important for modesty.** Every man and every lady should be concerned about modesty. I Timothy 2 teaches that modesty in a lady is a sign of submission to the Lord and is placed in the context of her prayers. The Bible teaches that dress is either immodest or modest. The Bible mentions the attire of a harlot, which is dressing in a provocative manner.

3) **Dress reveals a distinction between the genders.** Usually people identify gender by the way a person dresses. Hair also falls into this category. For a man to have long hair is an embarrassment and a shame, but a lady's hair is a covering given to her by God. Women who want to mix the genders oftentimes wear their hair in a traditional man's haircut, while men who struggle in this area will grow their hair long.

4) **Dress displays a testimony.** How you dress says something to an unsaved world. Every Christian needs to have an understanding of Christ-honoring dress and its relationship to his testimony. If you have ever seen Orthodox Jewish women, you will see that they wear dresses and modest skirts even though they are not Christians. Those who follow the Old Testament laws dress modestly and appropriately. Christians ought to do the very same and adhere to the biblical principle.

My wife and I invited a group of Hyles-Anderson College students to our house for an activity. While we were playing a game of volleyball in the park area across the street from our home, we were having a great time laughing and enjoying the game. A family from our neighborhood happened to walk by, so we waved at them. A few days later, they stopped by and knocked on our door. They said, "We have children, and we live in the neighborhood. We walked by here and saw such wholesome young people. They all were so distinctively different; their laughter and their dress told us that they were Christians. We saw that you have an older teenage daughter. Would your daughter consider watching our children?"

Our daughter has now regularly watched their children as a direct result of what they saw—the testimony of the Lord and the dress of the young people. Dress is very important to a person's Christian testimony.

Teach the ladies in your household to be proper Christian ladies in their attitudes (how they respond), in their actions (how they conduct themselves), in their modesty (how they dress) and in their speech (how they talk).

3.
TEACH YOUR CHILDREN THAT WHITE STANDS FOR PURITY.

I WILL NEVER forget my dad's stressing, "Remember, white at your wedding stands for purity." Ecclesiastes 9:8 says, *"Let thy garments be always white...."* White is also a festive color. Oftentimes, people will wear white or lighter colors on Resurrection Sunday.

White is a color of rejoicing that also depicts purity. Living a pure life is for both the young lady and the young man. *"Let no man despise thy youth; but be thou an example of the unbelievers, in word, in conversation, in charity, in spirit, in faith, in purity"* (I Timothy 4:12).

Paul also stressed to Timothy, *"...keep thyself pure"* (I Timothy 5:22).

4.
TEACH YOUR CHILDREN
TO BE THEMSELVES.

M Y DAD DID not like hypocrisy, and he didn't like any of his children putting on an act. I can still hear him say, "I want you to be yourself, but I want you to be the best self that you possibly can be." Psalm 139:14 says, *"I will praise thee for I am fearfully and wonderfully made: marvelous are thy works; and that my soul knoweth right well."* My dad oftentimes complimented his children on their strengths, but he did not allow us to compare ourselves among ourselves.

Though I was older, my brother Matthew was a much better athlete than I was. For a while, he was even taller than I was. Having my little brother taller used to drive me crazy! When we played basketball, he would start on the first five, and I would be the sixth man off the bench. I remember having long talks on the way home with my dad when I would be tearful and frustrated. "Dad, what's the coach see in Matt that he doesn't see in me?"

He would wisely answer, "John, you're different. You're special. Be the best John you can be. Don't try to be Matt. Don't try to impress other people. Just be yourself and let God use you to do that."

My dad always gave me such great advice. Parents, let your children be themselves. Teach them to be who they are. Comparing ourselves is not wise. Many kids get into trouble because they're trying to be somebody else or they are trying to keep up with someone else. When that young person comes to the realization that he can't perform like others can, remind him that God made him special and different—like my father did for me.

Children need to learn to be themselves while they are children so if they are in a ministry position, such as a pastor, they won't feel the need to compare themselves to someone else. Because people are different, they will have strengths where others have weaknesses. God makes some people good in certain areas and others good in different areas. Comparison is brutal, and God wants us to refrain from the practice of comparing. *"For we dare not make ourselves of the number, or compare ourselves with some that commend themselves: but they measuring themselves by themselves, and comparing themselves among themselves, are not wise"* (II Corinthians 10:12).

5.
GIVE CHILDREN CHORES AND RESPONSIBILITIES.

INSIST THAT YOUR children do a good, thorough job. First teach them how to do each job; don't expect them to know how. Proverbs 22:29 says, *"Seest thou a man diligent in his business? he shall stand before kings...."* Proverbs 22:6, *"Train up a child in the way he should go...."*

As I pondered how to illustrate this proverb from my father, I thought about the time I chipped a tooth playing ice hockey at the Little Red Barn Skating Rink in Superior, Wisconsin. A guy got upset and threw his stick at my mouth, chipping my front tooth. I promise, I kept my mouth shut all the way home! Have you ever had the misfortune of chipping a tooth? Then you know the feeling. Anytime I opened my mouth and cool air hit that tooth, the only way I can describe the feeling is that my head felt like it was going to blow up.

I began thinking about Proverbs 25:19, which says, *"Confidence in an unfaithful man in time of trouble is like a broken tooth, and a foot out of joint."* If your ankle is sprained, the whole body is crippled. That's exactly how it is when someone does not finish a job. Doing chores and responsibilities well takes time, but it teaches character.

6.
LET YOUR CHILDREN PLAY SPORTS.

A S CHILDREN ARE playing sports, teach them to keep a strong Christian testimony. Because my dad enjoyed sports, the Wilkerson kids would participate in whatever the sport of the season was. Some of my siblings were fairly good athletes, but I felt I was merely another warm body on the team most of the time.

Proverbs 16:32 says, *"He that is slow to anger is better than the mighty; and he that ruleth his spirit than he that taketh a city."* Dad wanted his children to play football hard and play to win. If someone fell down on the football field, the soccer field, or the basketball court, he would insist that we try to help them up. If the ball traveled out of bounds, he would insist that we go pick up the ball for the referee. If we fouled another player, we were to raise our hand and admit to committing the foul. He would say, "If you didn't foul and if the referee points to you and calls your number, raise your hand and be respectful." He wanted us to learn to keep our temper in check.

I will admit that I don't play sports simply to get exercise; I play because I like to win. I seriously want to win every time I play. I don't care if I'm playing a star athlete or if I'm playing my sister; I want to win! That's why treadmills frustrate me. Give me a tennis court and give me somebody with whom to compete! Nonetheless, parents, teach your children to play sports, and teach them to control their attitude.

I personally believe sports are wonderful. However, most young men also need to learn some sort of musical instrument or to use whatever musical ability they have in some way. I love to see young men who sing, but I also love to see them on the athletic field. Musically gifted young men don't have to be all-star athletes, but they should participate. All-star athletes don't have to sing a solo or earn first chair in the orchestra, but they ought to take part in a music program. Every young person should be balanced in these areas.

Learning sports has a way of promoting balance. Sports can add some good discipline to a person's life and also reveal some of his worst characteristics. Different sports teach different attributes. Those who wrestle must learn self-discipline. Those who play baseball or basketball or another team sport can face a pressure cooker of rejection, disappointment, victory, and camaraderie. In every situation, an athlete should have a Christian spirit and learn to control his temper and attitude. *"He that hath no rule over his own spirit is like a city that is broken down, and without walls"* (Proverbs 25:28).

Athletics has a way of teaching a young person to control his attitude. Having a Christian spirit can be challenging. It's not natural for a person to control his temper; it's natural for him to lose his temper. It's natural to become angry and frustrated and to experience pain when someone elbows you in the nose. Be a good testimony at all costs—not because of the coach or because of the school, but because of Jesus!

7.
TEACH YOUR CHILDREN TO BE GOOD SPORTS OR DON'T PLAY.

IN OTHER WORDS, learn to control your temper on the court or field. Because I grew up loving sports, I love to see young men play sports. Recently I was watching the youth sing for a program, and I enjoyed watching several young people who were blending music and athletics in their lives. I love to see young people who excel in both music and athletics.

I know an unbelievable pianist who in his youth purposely decided to become an athlete. Though he was never the best player on the court, he worked hard to learn to dribble a basketball; he learned how to throw a football and catch it. I believe this tenacity made him a valuable servant of God and someone who is now highly respected. Learn to be good at different disciplines, adding to your toolbox. The person who says, "I'm only good in this area, so that's all I'm going to learn" will limit how he is used long-term.

Parents, help your children diversify. If they only excel in one area and that skill is no longer needed, then they will struggle in life.

I once heard an employee say, "I don't want to learn anything because I might be asked to do it." That person has ultimately placed a cap on his abilities. The attitude this person has displayed his whole life has been, "I'm going to get by with the least I can do. I don't want anyone to know I can do anything." I have watched that man struggle financially and with his family because of laziness.

Not too long ago, I was watching some young people play basketball. Whenever they didn't get what they wanted, I noticed they slammed the ball down really hard or they argued with the referee. They lost their tempers whenever they did something wrong or when they felt someone had wronged them. The attitude "It's all about ME!" showed all over them. I am all for competitiveness, but young people need to keep their tempers in check. I well remember the times my dad would cloud up and rain all over his children when we lost our tempers. We would receive a lecture all the way home, and oftentimes when we arrived home, he dealt with us individually—not pleasantly, I might add.

Proverbs 12:16 says, *"A fool's wrath is presently known: but a prudent man covereth shame."* When a fool is angry, everybody knows because he makes sure everybody knows. He kicks a chair. He yells. He snarls. He hits. He stomps. But a prudent man covers the embarrassment of that anger. Many know the name Bobby Knight for one reason—temper tantrums. This unbelievable coach will always be remembered for throwing a chair across the basketball court. Woody Hayes, one of Ohio State University's great coaches, once grabbed hold of an opposing player, slapped him, and punched him. Why? Because he lost his temper.

Anyone can enjoy sports while keeping his temper under control. Don't lose your temper. There's nothing manly about losing your temper on a basketball floor or volleyball court or on the soccer field.

Proverbs 16:32, *"He that is slow to anger is better than the mighty; and he that ruleth his spirit than he that taketh a city."*

Proverbs 19:11, *"The discretion of a man deferreth his anger; and it is his glory to pass over a transgression."* The Bible says a man's discretion (showing good judgment) holds his anger in check.

Proverbs 15:1, *"A soft answer turneth away wrath...."*

One of my favorite verses on anger is James 1:20, *"For the wrath of man worketh not the righteousness of God."* In and of itself, anger is not a sin. God gets angry with a righteous indignation. However, most of the time, anger crosses over into an out-of-control area of wrath. When an angry man will not do what God wants him to do, he starts saying things he shouldn't say. He tries to hurt people or himself. He hurts his future and complicates life. Eventually, he embarrasses himself, but a prudent man covers the embarrassment of those reactions.

Parents must also teach their children to defer anger. God lets those who keep their temper under control do more and have more influence.

8.
Do not put your children on a pedestal.

Sometimes leaders can be guilty of putting their children on a pedestal. You have likely met someone who thought his kid could do no wrong. Parents of "perfect" children usually are very embarrassed at some point because their children are exactly like their parents—they are "stinkers." Every child has issues, just as his parents have issues. Children need a dad and a mom to discipline them, work with them, and challenge them to be and do better. The truth of the matter is that parents need to praise their kids, not put them on a pedestal. The power of praise cannot be calculated.

Don't become defensive when your child is corrected. Far too many parents hurt their children when their children are corrected. Instead of standing by the authority, those parents become critical of the leader. They assert their right to be defensive by declaring, "I'm a mom; I protect my kids!"

I certainly understand a parent's desire to protect his children, but sometimes parents erroneously believe and state, "My child would never do that." Parents, don't put your children on a pedestal; you never know what they are capable of doing. You'll find out from a district attorney or a police detective what they could do if you're not careful in that area. Praise and encourage your children, but be careful about putting them on a pedestal.

In churches where my parents and siblings were members, my dad would sign up our family to be the church janitors. Today I thank God for this opportunity because Dad taught us to do our jobs thoroughly. I don't think I'm exaggerating in saying I have cleaned church auditoriums and church bathrooms hundreds of times. I've probably mopped many square miles of fellowship halls and hallways. I have stripped and waxed floors. I have gathered the trash and picked up trash all around the church property. I have cleaned up an overabundance of other people's messes. I cannot imagine someone's sticking a piece of bubblegum underneath his or her seat. I cannot fathom someone's leaving trash in the songbook rack. If the trash is overflowing in the bathroom, pick it up and push it down. We should determine to be a cleaning crew of one. Why?

- I wouldn't want anyone to think that I left it that way. That's probably prideful, but I always keep that thought in mind.

- I feel that the church facility is God's house, and I need to do my best to help take care of His house. My dad always wanted to make sure we respected the church building and property.

Cleaning buses is another thankless chore but one that needs attention. One of the last tasks our son Tyler did before he went to heaven was to clean out a church bus that had returned from camp. When he and his brother Derrick got home, the two boys swept and mopped the bus, emptied the trash can, and prepared the bus for the Sunday morning service.

Those kinds of tasks help teach a young person humility and keep him grounded. Someone said, "Stay low; no one ever fell off the floor." Stay humble.

Parents must "keep it real" with their kids. They cannot

afford to defend them and say, "Well, my kids would never do that" or "I'm not going to make them clean up other people's messes." My friend, you might want to have them clean up other people's messes; it would help them not to leave a mess for other people and would awaken them to the reality of Christian leadership.

Years ago my mother used to say, "Son, I'm going to love you no matter what. I want to rear you so the whole world will love you." I don't want to rear kids just so I'll love them because I'll love them no matter what. If my children become a prisoner or a president, I will love them. I want to rear children that the whole world will love, but that doesn't happen when they are put on a pedestal. Teaching children discipline and humility will result in their being loved.

> Proverbs 25:6, 7, *"Put not forth thyself in the presence of the king, and stand not in the place of great men: ⁷For better it is that it be said unto thee, Come up hither; than that thou shouldest be put lower in the presence of the prince whom thine eyes have seen."*

The principle being taught in this Scripture is that it is better to come from the bottom than to be placed in a position and fall because the character needed to fulfill that position is lacking. Saul and Rehoboam are examples of men who had a position, but they didn't have the character to stay in that position. Starting on the ground floor and coming up through the ranks is better than being given an unearned position. Guard against the temptation of putting your children on a pedestal.

In I Peter 5:1-3, the apostle Peter, under the inspiration of the Holy Spirit of God, gave pastors advice about how to be a pastor.

"The elders which are among you I exhort, who am also an elder, and a witness of the sufferings of Christ, and also a partaker of the glory that shall be revealed: ²Feed the flock of God which is among you, taking the oversight thereof, not by constraint, but willingly; not for filthy lucre, but of a ready mind; ³Neither as being lords over God's heritage, but being ensamples to the flock."

Peter is telling pastors to feed the flock of God—not because they have to for a paycheck but because God put in their hearts a willingness to pastor. He tells every pastor, every youth pastor, every Sunday school teacher, and anyone who is shepherding people to take ownership and the responsibility for what God has called them to do. The apostle tells them not to pastor as a lord or as a boss over God's heritage, but they are to pastor as an example to the flock.

Verse 4 adds, *"And when the chief Shepherd [Jesus] shall appear, ye shall receive a crown of glory that fadeth not away."* I have the joy of pastoring a church, but biblically, two positions are available in Christianity:

1) Serving as the pastor of a Bible-believing church

2) Helping the pastor to pastor a Bible-believing church.

Church members need to find out where they fit in the body and help the pastor. Every pastor needs help to pastor people.

I cannot pastor the two- and three-year-old toddlers at church, but they do have a leader who is an extension of the pastoral ministry in that class. I cannot preach the morning service and also lead the junior church for the "B," "C," and "D" bus children who meet in other facilities on Sunday morning, but thankfully, someone else has found his place in that area of responsibility. Our Spanish pastor serves as an extension of the pastoral ministry to the Spanish congregation.

> I Peter 5:5, 6, *"Likewise,* [in the same way] *ye younger, submit yourself unto the elder. Yea, all of you be subject one to another, and be clothed with humility: for God resisteth the proud, and giveth grace to the humble. ⁶Humble yourselves therefore under the mighty hand of God, that he may exalt you in due time."*

In these two verses, Peter was addressing those who were in the family—the teenagers and children. They are to come underneath the authority in their lives while they are young. They are to learn to submit and to be humble. Young people must learn to be submissive because God is watching for submissive young people, not rebels. A *rebel* is somebody who thinks he or she is in control and free, but the truth of the matter is that a rebel is like a Chihuahua on a choke chain being jerked around by Satanic influences. Rebellious people are frustrated, wondering what happened to them.

The Bible says rebellion is like the sin of witchcraft (I Samuel 15:23). I don't know about you, but I want to be wherever witchcraft, séances, devil worship, and demonology are *not*. However, when we are rebellious against our God-given authority, we open doors in our lives that allow demonic influences and temptation.

Don't put your kids on a pedestal! Instead, help them to stay low. Help them to grow up with hard work, discipline, submission. Point them toward the practice of showing support for their authorities. Don't allow them to pit Mom and Dad against each other—a tactic kids will naturally try. Teach them to submit to their parents and teachers at school. Be very careful about running to their aid and trying to fill their every need, want, and desire. Every child needs to learn to be humble, submissive, and obedient rather than being placed on a pedestal where they will eventually fall. Putting children on a pedestal will embarrass them and you; they will fall. They need to be reared in humility.

I Peter 5:5, 6, "...*God resisteth the proud, and giveth grace to the humble. Humble yourselves therefore under the mighty hand of God, that he may exalt you in due time.*" God wants to bless His children. He wants to help them grow in their spiritual influence and nature. Help them to grow by loving them. If someone praises your kids, say, "God's so good to them."

I heard people say to my dad many times, "Your kids are great."

He would always say, "It's by the grace of God. Only by the grace of God." His response would probably be a good response today. Thank God for His goodness. Keep praying for your children. We are to love them because we want the Lord to use them.

9.

TEACH YOUR CHILDREN TO BE CONTENT EVERYWHERE WITH EVERYTHING.

CONTENTMENT MUST BE learned. Being content can be challenging for husbands, for wives, for parents, and for children. We live in a world where everything beckons to us saying, "You don't have enough." "You don't have a good life." "You need to be happy." "You'll only be happy if you have this, this, and this." Billboards and advertisements continually bombard us with what we need.

Today's video games are designed to make the player discontent as he conquers one level. He then wants to buy the next level. The game is constructed so the player continues to become disenfranchised and discontented with what he has. He needs more bells and whistles to continue playing. What happens? A mindset of needing more new and more exciting things is created. This mindset will impact marriages. When you are not happy in your marriage, you want out to do something else.

Learning to be content everywhere with everything is very challenging. Philippians 4:10 says, *"But I rejoiced in the Lord greatly, that now at the last your care of me hath flourished again; wherein ye were also careful, but ye lacked opportunity."* Paul was writing to a church that had supported him as a missionary.

Verses 11-13 continue, *"Not that I speak in respect of want: for I have learned, in whatsoever state I am, therewith to be content. I know both how to be abased, and I know how to abound: every where and in all things I am instructed both to be full and to be hungry, both to abound and to suffer need. I can do all things through Christ which strengtheneth me."*

What do these verses mean? Using a simplistic illustration, you can't win every basketball game you play. You cannot conquer every foe you have. What the verse does mean is that you can do anything that God wants you to do. You can go on in the good times and in the bad times. You can be content with little or with a lot. You can be content everywhere and with everything.

When I was growing up, my dad would say a thousand times (or so it seemed): "Eat what's on your plate." We were not allowed to get up from the table and leave any food on our plates. Saying, "I don't care for macaroni and cheese" was not tolerated. The fact that I didn't care for it didn't matter; when my mother served it, I was going to eat it, compliments of Dad.

To this day, mac and cheese is not one of my favorites, but whatever Mom put on the table, I was taught to eat. I could always tell when my dad was running out of money; we would have what Dad called "cowboy stew." Every leftover in the whole refrigerator went into one pot. He said, "Cowboy stew! Come on, now, everyone, roundup! Let's go."

"No, Dad, no!" we would all protest in unison.

"Let me go to a friend's house," I would say. That plan to avoid cowboy stew worked when I was six and seven, but when I was a teenager, it no longer worked.

Once when my family was at the bottom of the barrel,

mackerel patties were the main course. I have eaten my fair share of mackerel patties because my dad had a rule: "Whatever we have is what we're going to eat."

I learned very quickly to be content everywhere with everything. Know that God has given you everything you need to be happy right now. Whatever you need is exactly what God has given you.

10.

TEACH YOUR CHILDREN THAT LITTLE THINGS ARE IMPORTANT.

T HE SONG SAYS, "Little is much when God is in it!" Luke 16 contains the story of the unjust steward who did not do a good job in taking care of his owner's property. When he was about to lose his job, he devised a plan to make friends by brokering deals with his employer's debtors while he awaited dismissal from his stewardship. The adjustments the steward made earned his owner's commendation. Basically, in a limited amount of time, he made some fairly shrewd decisions at his employer's expense, but he made both himself and his boss popular with their clients. The unjust steward was deemed wiser in his generation than the children of light. Then Jesus said, *"Make to yourselves friends of the mammon of unrighteousness; that, when ye fail* [when you die or are dismissed from the stewardship of life], *they may receive you into everlasting habitations."*

One reason why I encourage people to give faithfully to missions and spread the gospel of salvation is that they will make friends in this lifetime. Media, material, and men are all financed by money, and all are expedient in reaching the souls of men.

Try doing some little things for your neighbors. During the holidays, remember them with a small gift. Prepare an extra tray of food and take it to them. No one has enough money to feed the neighborhood, but occasionally we should be a blessing to somebody else. Little things do matter to God.

Luke 16:10 says, *"He that is faithful in that which is least is faithful also in much: and he that is unjust in the least is unjust also in much."* The word *faithful* is key to understanding this verse. God says when someone is faithful in the little things, then he will be given more things with which to be faithful. If the person is careless in the little matters, he will not be given more responsibilities to oversee.

The importance of little things is taught in the Bible and has been taught by great men and ladies of God. My father emphasized giving attention to the small things. "Take care of how you dress," he would say. "If you use the restroom and find a mess, do the small thing and pick up the litter. If you are at church, leave your pew the way you found it or better. Pick up any trash in the area where you sat."

We may think or maybe even say, "That's the janitor's job; he is paid to clean."

We must guard against such thinking! *"For the ways of man are before the eyes of the LORD, and he pondereth all his goings"* (Proverbs 5:21). God is watching everything we do. After all, He's an investor—the greatest one, I might add. *"The eyes of the LORD run to and fro throughout the whole earth, to shew himself strong in the behalf of them whose heart is perfect toward him..."* (2 Chronicles 16:9). He is always looking at our hearts, and He knows our attitude.

Luke 16:11 continues, *"If therefore ye have not been faithful in the unrighteous mammon* [money, finances, possessions], *who will commit to your trust the true riches?"* Money can buy a bed, but it can't buy sleep. Money can pay for a beautiful wedding, but it cannot guarantee a beautiful marriage. Money can do many things, but it cannot give you power with God nor influence for the souls of men and women, boys and girls. Only God can give you this power. God watches how we use the money He has given us, and He also gives us that which money cannot buy. Only God can give true riches—intangible gifts of His Spirit.

Luke 16:12, *"And if ye have not been faithful in that which is another man's, who shall give you that which is your own?"* In this verse, God gives the principle that if we are not careful with the things of others, He cannot bless us with our own.

I cannot express enough the importance of being mindful of helping our children do the little things. If you ask your child to make the bed, then by all means insist that he make the bed! Saying, "No one sleeps there but me" is unacceptable. If you ask your child to clean his room, then see that it is cleaned! Don't allow your children to be careless. Making sure everything has a place and everything is in its place is a good rule to follow.

Try to be aware of the small things in life. When you take your children out to eat, make sure you leave the table clean and the chairs pushed back in. Don't frequent a restaurant with your family and leave a Gospel tract or talk to someone about Christ if you leave the place looking like a pigsty. Take the time to stack your cups and plates in an orderly manner and gather the silverware together.

Why? Because little things are important, and we are not representing ourselves. We are representing God, and we need to be a good testimony for Christ. I am well aware that the waitress and busboys are paid to clean up. I know cleaning up may seem like a small, inconsequential matter, but being courteous is a big matter—especially when leaving a Gospel tract with a tip inside. Your courtesy may be used to love that person to the Lord Jesus Christ.

11.
TEACH CHILDREN TO WORK.

THE BIBLICAL PRINCIPLE is, "If you don't work, you don't eat." II Thessalonians 3:10 reminds us that if a man doesn't work, neither should he eat.

> Proverbs 6:6-11, *"Go to the ant, thou sluggard; consider her ways, and be wise: Which having no guide, overseer, or ruler, Provideth her meat in the summer, and gathereth her food in the harvest. How long wilt thou sleep, O sluggard? when wilt thou arise out of thy sleep? Yet a little sleep, a little slumber, a little folding of the hands to sleep: So shall thy poverty come as one that travelleth, and thy want as an armed man."*

In this passage, Solomon is saying to his son, "If you are lazy, go watch an ant." Ants aren't found kicking back under a bamboo tree drinking iced tea. Ants are industrious members of the insect world. Most of the ants we see are female ants, which is why the Bible uses the pronoun *her*. Solomon advised his son to watch her work. An ant doesn't have a drill sergeant running beside her, shouting instructions. She doesn't have a fellow ant urging her to work harder. Something is intrinsically inside of the ant that says, "I have to get going; winter's coming. I must store enough food in the summertime to last through winter."

Solomon uses the illustration of the ant to warn against laziness, which will bring about poverty and the need to ask others for assistance. Lazy people who constantly need help think nothing of asking other people to meet their needs for them. Eventually their neediness will wear out those who give.

I have discovered that people who hold signs asking for help and people who beg are generally always on the move. If you look for them in six months, you won't find them; they won't be in the same place. Having worn out their welcome, they will have moved on, looking for another benevolent soul to minister to them somewhere else. They move on to another place in another city because people get tired of continually helping—when laziness proves to be the problem.

I do realize that not everyone who has a need is lazy. The truth is that all of us will have a need at some time. As a rule, a lazy person stays on the move. Lazy people will resort to force, deceit, or fraud to get what they need or want. As an armed man, they'll resort to doing whatever they have to because after a while, benevolence won't work. To get what they want, lazy people will use illegal means. Ephesians 4:28, *"Let him that stole steal no more: but rather let him labour, working with his hands the thing which is good, that he may have to give to him that needeth."* Instead of stealing, lazy person, work with your own hands to obtain what you need, making sure your word is good, i.e., providing goods or a product of your work.

God blesses honest people so they can raise their standard of living as well as raise their standard of giving. If you are a giver, have you ever wondered why you seem to have a little more? God is trying to tell you that you are now taken care of, so help somebody else. The Lord often impresses my heart to help someone, and generally we have a little extra because my wife is extremely frugal. The fact that we can sometimes help somebody is probably why we have extra on occasion. However, the Bible also says, *"There is treasure to be desired and oil in the dwelling of the wise; but a foolish man spendeth it up"* (Proverbs 21:20). We should also learn to save.

God loves a cheerful giver, so learn to be a funnel and not a bucket. Be a channel, not a can. Learn the priceless truth that God can give through you what He will not give to you. Oftentimes in the name of saving, we want to hold tightly to what we have when we ought to learn to say, "I'll give."

All of us have a desire to do, to be, and to have. If we did not have that desire, we would just be a big blob sitting idle and accomplishing nothing. But God put inside of us inertia to have things, to do things, and to be something. A little girl growing up wants to be a wife and mother someday because she will have someone or several someones to help and shape and encourage. As a mother, she has a responsibility and a domain. Usually a wife has a little house or an apartment with a kitchen that is her kitchen. She controls what meals will be served. Moms determine how the kids will be cared for and what time they are going to bed. Making these decisions is part of her need, and nothing is wrong with that.

A boy grows up dreaming of getting a good job and going to work. In his dreams he would like to be someone who could make decisions for what his workplace will be like. Many times those childhood dreams come true! Sometimes something inside a man says, "I want to be the boss." Why? Because God built within every person the desire to be, to do, and to have.

Obviously, we can go overboard in fulfilling these three needs, so God provided an antidote for each one. God's antidote to materialism is to give. The antidote to being in charge is to pray. God's antidote to doing what I want to do is to fast (Matthew 6).

My first job was loading bricks on a backhoe. A building was being destroyed in our neighborhood, and my dad talked the owner into hiring my brother and me to load bricks on the backhoe. All day long we piled bricks on the backhoe, and when we had a load, the backhoe operator would dump them where they needed to be.

Our next job was picking up trash in a mall parking lot. When I was in third grade and my brother was in second grade, we had a job cleaning the fountains in the mall parking lot. If child labor laws were in existence then, my dad knew nothing about them! I wasn't very happy then, but I am very grateful to this day that he taught me to work hard.

Dad expected his sons to work hard. One day I made the mistake of telling my dad, "Dad, I'm bored. There's nothing to do."

He said, "I can fix that all right." I was soon cleaning out gutters and washing windows—for free, no less! I believe that was the last time I ever got bored because Dad was a master at finding something for me to do.

"If you're bored, son, we can fix…" Dad fixed my attitude, and in fixing my attitude, I found out that working hard brings blessing. The harder I work, the more blessed I am.

Many people say, "You are so lucky." The child who learns to love work will carry that love through adulthood. The professional golfer who wins the PGA Championship worked hard for that title; he is not lucky. Thomas Jefferson is credited with saying, "I'm a great believer in luck, and I find the harder I work, the more I have of it." I don't personally believe in luck; I believe in being blessed. I have found that the harder I work, the more God blesses me.

12.
WORK TOGETHER TILL JESUS COMES.

I CORINTHIANS 15:58 SAYS, *"Therefore, my beloved brethren, be ye stedfast, unmoveable, always abounding in the work of the Lord, forasmuch as ye know that your labour is not in vain in the Lord."* Get the family involved in the Lord's work together. John C. Maxwell, the leadership guru, said, "Teamwork makes the dream work." Realize that God allows us to do more together than we can do as one person. Many hands make for light work.

Another thought that comes to my mind in regard to working together is *synergy*, which means "the whole effort" accomplishes more than any one individual part. Synergy is a great concept in learning to work together as a family.

During our church's Saturday soul-winning meeting, I encourage entire families—mom, dad, and the kids—to go together to knock on doors and witness to people. I love it whenever entire families work on a bus route together. Dr. Pete Cowling's entire family works on bus routes. On any given Sunday, he will testify, "Every one of my grandkids served on a bus route last week." The Cowlings are a family working together for the cause of Christ.

My dad made sure his children did something to serve the Lord. Usually when we went to church, my dad volunteered us to be the janitors of the church. Every Saturday of the world we were at the church. We would go to the soul-winning meeting if they had one. If they didn't have one, we would still go to the church to go on visitation. That afternoon Dad would get the family together, and we would clean the fellowship hall, wipe down the chairs, straighten the songbooks, and pick up any paper we found in the auditorium. Cleaning numerous auditoriums cured me of leaving my trash—ever. I did not want someone else to have to clean up for me. My siblings are the same way, and we are that way because of my dad's insistence that we clean up after ourselves. I thank God that my dad took me along on the journey of serving the Lord with him.

He always involved his children in multiple ways at church. My father would challenge me and almost force me to do things I did not want to do until I did them, and then I was glad he had challenged me. I rode my first church bus route as a "worker" when I was about nine years old. Dad wanted me to lead the singing on the bus, but I didn't want to do that.

My dad told the bus captain to have me lead the singing. "John is good at singing," he said.

I protested, "Dad, I can't do that."

Dad didn't listen to me. He just said, "Yes, you can."

I didn't like it then when Dad volunteered me, but I'm grateful that he took me along on that journey of learning to serve. He worked with my brothers and me to help us become better songleaders by teaching us a beat pattern with the song's rhythm—something he had learned in college. How thankful I am that as a young boy, Dad challenged me to climb to new heights for the Lord Jesus Christ.

Abounding in the work of the Lord became a part of us. Serving wasn't something we watched everyone else do; our family served together. If the church had a work day, everybody in the family was going.

In I Corinthians 16:15, the apostle Paul was closing this letter and he wrote, *"I beseech you, brethren, (ye know the house of Stephanas, that it is the firstfruits* [one of the first families to be saved in Corinth] *of Achaia, and that they have addicted themselves to the ministry of the saints)."* Stephanas and his family were biblical examples of people who had learned to serve those around them together as a family.

Many times children and young people do not like to serve others. I have taken my family to a nursing home a number of times because I believe visiting nursing homes teaches our children that the work of the Lord is work. The family of Stephanas was always involved in the work of the Lord. God commended them by saying they were addicted to helping people. This verse is the only place in the Bible where the word *addicted* is found. Today people are addicted to everything from pornography to gambling to Twinkies, but God wants us to be addicted to ministry—to people.

So many times when I was growing up, my dad would hear of a need. Perhaps a widow needed someone to take care of her lawn. Dad would always say, "John, Matt, you guys take care of that."

"Well, how much are we going to get?"

"You'll get your reward in Heaven. Go over there and get that done."

I often chafed at his reply, but I am so glad he taught me to work and to care about others. Let's minister together; let's work together for the cause of Christ.

John 9:4 addresses the principle of working together until Jesus comes. I am not what I ought to be, but I can testify that so many things in my life have been blessed because of hard work. Author and educator, Dr. Tom Vogel, is known for saying, "He who does the work does the learning." In other words, whenever people do the work, they learn how to do the work.

In just a few days, we all will stand before the Judgment Seat of Christ and give an account for the things we've done while we walked this earth. Jesus said in John 9:4, *"I must work the works of him that sent me, while it is day: the night cometh, when no man can work."* Get involved in working together as a family.

In John 5:17, Jesus says, *"...My Father worketh hitherto, and I work."* I love reading that passage and considering how Jesus was saying, "I'm emulating My Dad. My Father worked, and I also work." Learn to work together as a family until Jesus comes.

13.
TEACH YOUR CHILDREN TO STRIVE FOR CONSISTENCY AND TO BE A GOOD EXAMPLE.

M OST PARENTS WOULD agree that one of the most difficult disciplines is to be consistent. I have found that inconsistency and hypocrisy probably do more to provoke children to anger than anything else. When we are one way at church and another way at home, the inconsistency drives a wedge between parents and children. That kind of behavior causes frustration in the lives of young people.

My father's last entry in his proverbs for parents was to work to be consistent. Being consistent is no easy task, but one that the Spirit of God helps us with. Ephesians 6:4, *"And, ye fathers, provoke not your children to wrath: but bring them up in the nurture and admonition of the Lord."* Work hard not to make your children angry or provoke them to wrath. The antidote for wrath is found in Proverbs 15:1, which says, *"A soft answer turneth away wrath...."*

Colossians 3:21 says, *"Fathers, provoke not your children to anger, lest they be discouraged."* Discouragement has a way of really sapping a young person. You can see the discouragement in the eyes of a young person. Sometimes discouragement comes because of the absence of a father. The Devil works hard to see that fathers are angry, abusive, addicted, aloof, or absent altogether, which can bring great frustration in the life of a child and ultimately discourage him.

Obviously, no father is perfect. No parent is perfect. Some kids think, "When I'm a dad..." or "When I'm a mom...." After fifteen years, check back and tell us how you are doing in the parenting process!

Start praying and asking God for His help now. Say, "Lord, with Your help I want to be the dad You want me to be someday. I want to be consistent. I want to be faithful." Consistency and balance are the keys to a Spirit-filled life. Say, "God, I want to be Spirit-filled."

I don't always do this, but often before I walk through the door of my house, I hold the handle a little longer and pray, "Lord, help me to be Spirit-filled because I don't know what's happening on the other side of this door. I don't know what's going on inside the hearts of our kids. I don't know what they need. I don't know what they have experienced. I don't know what Linda needs, but help me to be Spirit-filled so I know how to be what each of them needs."

I want to always provide a good example for my family.

CHRISTIAN
TESTIMONY

Be dogmatically true,
obstinately holy,
immovably honest,
desperately kind,
fixed upright.

– Charles Spurgeon

1.
EMPHASIZE MISSIONS
OR WORLD EVANGELISM.

SOON AFTER MY dad's salvation, his heart was touched for missions. I do not find it surprising that my sister Janna is a missionary, and as far as I know, every one of his children give regularly to faith promise missions. Many of his grandkids have already visited the mission field before their twenty-first birthday to serve in missionary work. I am relatively sure that others will do the same in due time.

My father attended Baptist Bible College in Springfield, Missouri, a school that sent out many great missionaries. Anytime a missionary visited our church, we were there for the slide presentation. He would often speak to the pastor about letting the missionary come to our house to eat or spend the night. My parents used our house as a hospitality center even though we really had the poorest of places.

To this day, I thank the Lord for my father's emphasis on world evangelism. Because my dad was faithful to take me to churches that were missions-minded, I began to give systematically to world evangelism, as a seventeen-year-old boy. Every week I gave five dollars, and then every year after, with the exception of one, I have tried to increase my giving over the last 30-plus years. I know I owe a lot of that commitment to my dad because he kept missions in front of me. *"Go ye into all the world and preach the gospel to every creature"* (Mark 16:15).

To this day, every time there's a missions conference, I want all of my children to attend. Every Sunday morning, they get their offerings ready to give to world evangelism—just like my parents encouraged me to do. Perhaps they are not necessarily as systematic as they will become one day, but an emphasis on missions will move their hearts in that direction.

2.
TEACH CHILDREN EARLY TO TITHE AND TO GIVE TO FAITH PROMISE MISSIONS.

ONE YEAR DURING a spring break from school, Northwest Indiana had a snowstorm. When I came home for supper, one of my sons was excited to tell me what he had spent the day doing. "Dad, in the last two days I've made $135 shoveling snow!" I was thrilled to think that our high school son had worked so hard. I was even happier to know that he would meet with his mom on Sunday morning to make sure he had $13.50 to give to God and $6.00 for his faith promise missions commitment!

Two things are required in order to tithe: arithmetic and obedience. Do the math and obey. Assess your increase, divide it by ten, bring it to church, and commit it to the Lord. My wife and I have encouraged our children to commit to give to missions. We want to encourage them not just to give the tithe, but to give above the tithe.

The tithe shows my honesty and my integrity with the Lord. The offering shows my love and my generosity. The offering shows that I get to give. I don't have to give an offering, but I get to because God loves me so much, and I love Him. I want Him to know how genuinely thankful I am.

I love that time of the year when the faith promise commitment cards are presented to the church family. Since 1984, when I was seventeen years old and someone handed me my first opportunity to give to faith promise missions, I have been taking a commitment card and promising God to give to missions. I filled it out the first time, promising to give $5 a week to missions. I think making that commitment is the third best decision of my life.

The first best decision was the night I was saved. The second best decision was surrendering my life to Him. I remember praying, "Lord, I belong to You; You belong to me. I want You to know I have You, and You have me. I'm surrendering my life to You."

I believe with all of my heart that I am married to the woman I'm married to because of giving to world evangelism. When I give to world evangelism, the Bible teaches that my God will supply all of my need (Philippians 4:19), and I am probably the most needy man on the planet.

Our church gives aggressively to missions because this church is a needy church. People note the big buildings, but a multitude of buildings means big bills. Yes, we have lots of people; we also have lots of problems. Our church and pastor need God more than we need anything on this planet. Thank God He will supply all of our need as we give to spread the gospel.

Every child needs to learn to give to missions. Young person, please don't wait until you graduate from high school to start giving. I missed all of those years of consistently giving to missions, quite frankly because I simply didn't know any better. Our churches did not encourage missions giving, or if they did, I missed its importance. I want to make sure all of the Wilkerson children "get it"; I want them to learn to be generous with God because He always blesses generosity, and He always condemns greed and selfishness. *"Give, and it shall be given unto you; good measure, pressed down, and shaken together, and running over, shall men give into your bosom. For with the same measure that ye mete withal it shall be measured to you again"* (Luke 6:38).

My dad was an extremely generous man, and I thank God that He gave me a dad who modeled giving. I didn't just hear about giving; I saw giving in action. God blessed my dad because of generosity. Our family learned together how to give. I learned it at the feet of my father, and I am very grateful for his example.

3.
EVERYONE SHOULD KNOW THAT YOU ARE A CHRISTIAN.

STRIVE TO HAVE a glass-house testimony. Proverbs 20:11 says, *"Even a child is known by his doings, whether his work be pure...."* If a man loves God, the same is known about him. Everyone should recognize that we are a child of God. Matthew 5:14, 15, *"Ye are the light of the world. A city that is set on an hill cannot be hid. Neither do men light a candle, and put it under a bushel...."* Sometimes people hide their "candle" at work, and the people with whom they work have no idea they are a Christian. Another place people sometimes hide their "candle" is during leisure times.

I heard a story about a family that was going on vacation, and the children had caught on that "we live one way at home, but when we're on vacation, we can live differently. We can dress differently. We can go to places we normally would not go because we're not at home; we're on vacation." May I remind you that all ground is holy ground; every bush is a burning bush. What you wouldn't normally do where you live shouldn't be done anyplace else.

We should strive to be consistent in the way we live our lives. Matthew 5:16 says, *"Let your light so shine before men, that they may see your good works, and glorify your Father which is in heaven."* If you are a Christian, everybody should know you're a Christian—especially those in your own household. I thank

God now that my dad was especially careful to be consistent, though I didn't like it sometimes when I was growing up.

When I was in the second grade, I was attending public school. One of the boys in my class wanted me to go to his birthday party, so my dad went to the store and bought him a football or something comparable. I was fine with that choice, but then my dad wanted to get him a Bible with his name imprinted on it. I did not like that idea because I was embarrassed. After all, I was in a public school, and I knew that gift would be a problem for me. I didn't know how my friend would handle that present, but my dad insisted on purchasing the Bible.

I remember crying and saying, "Dad, that's going to be so embarrassing!"

Dad took the time to sit down with me and explain his purpose. "Son, you're a Christian. Everybody should know that we're Christians, but not because we give him or her a Bible. People should recognize that we are Christians because of the way we act, the way we talk, and where we go. If you are a true friend, you should want your friend to know of Jesus."

In my own Adamic, sinful nature, I was embarrassed to be seen that way. Even with my dad's teaching fresh in my mind, I responded, "But, Dad, no one gets a Bible as a gift on his birthday." I had received Bibles, but I didn't think my unsaved friend would want a Bible.

My dad finally said, "John, either you will give him this Bible, or you're not going to the party." The discussion ended, he walked me into the friend's house, and I gave my friend two gifts instead of one. I will never forget my dad's saying that everyone needed to know I was a child of God. Everybody needs to know that I am a Christian, and Christians do live in glass houses.

Some people say, "I don't care what people think about me." My friend, you had better care because you are a direct reflection of the Lord Jesus Christ. How you dress, where you go, what you listen to, how you talk, how you conduct yourself, what your countenance reveals, and how you take care of your possessions are a reflection of Jesus Christ. Your yard is a reflection of Jesus Christ. Your vehicle is a reflection of Jesus Christ. You may not have a new vehicle, but you can keep that vehicle clean. You may not be able to dress with the expensive tastes of other people, but you can dress in an appropriate way. Your dress should say, "I'm a Christian; I'm a believer."

My dad insisted on our family's representing Christ well. A part of representing Christ well meant always being in church Sunday morning, Sunday evening, and Wednesday evening. Whether we were on vacation or at home, we were in a church someplace. I remember a time or two protesting: "Dad, let's skip Sunday school; let's just go to church."

"No, sir, John," he would respond. "You're going to be in a Sunday school class, and you will be a blessing and not a burden. You help make that class better by encouraging that teacher and the kids around you."

In this book, you will notice a common theme stressed multiple times—how thankful I am for my father's guidance though I didn't like it back then because I was sometimes embarrassed. Your children will one day be thankful for your guidance. The truth is, I was ashamed of the Lord Jesus Christ. I shouldn't have been, but I was because I didn't understand the big picture. But I'm glad my dad understood, and to this day, I appreciate his instruction.

4.
BE A BAPTIST BY CONVICTION.

M Y DAD WAS very strong on being a member of a fundamental, independent, Bible-believing, Baptist church because Baptist doctrine is Bible doctrine. Obviously, Baptist believers are not the only people going to Heaven. Other people throughout Christendom who do not attend Baptist churches believe in and accept Jesus Christ as their Saviour. God honors any Christian who honors Him.

I am grateful for the Baptist influence of my parents, but I am not a Baptist because my parents were. I am a Baptist because I began to study the history of Baptists and the biblical truths they have believed through the years.

A *conviction* is "knowing what you believe based upon Scripture." Everything we know, do, and practice should be from the Scriptures. The Scriptures should be our guiding tool because the Bible never changes. I change, my feelings change, society changes, culture changes, but the Bible is steady. *"The grass withereth, the flower fadeth: but the word of our God shall stand for ever"* (Isaiah 40:8). The Bible is an eternal Book forever settled in heaven (Psalm 119:89). The Scriptures lead us to principles, which lead us to convictions and decisions we must make.

Standards lead us to individual decisions that must be made for our practical life. I would like to reiterate that true Baptist doctrine is Bible doctrine. Simply because a church has "Baptist" on the sign does not mean that God wants us to attend that church or that the church believes these Bible principles.

Centuries ago, an established denomination in Europe grew tired of watching their people leave their denomination to become members of the Baptist faith. The hierarchy of that denomination decided to stop the egress and find a way to be rid of the Baptist believers. The authorities then sought the services of someone who would lead their charge to destroy the Baptists. After investigating, the person they sought to hire refused the job because he realized that stamping out the Baptist religion was impossible for three reasons:

1) **They were loyal to a Book—not a person.** If they were told to do something that went against the Bible, they would only do what the Bible told them to do.

2) **They did not remain in one place.** They continually sent out people because they believed their job was to tell the whole world the gospel of Christ and what the Bible said. The Baptists propagated what they believed was truth, and others embraced that truth.

3) **Those professing Baptists were good people, though not always understood.** Because they were responsible and respectable, trying to destroy them would fail. The people who lived in their community would likely defend them because they paid their bills, they cared for their property, and they were giving people who helped those having a hard time. The testimony of these people was above reproach.

Down through the ages, a group of people have always held to the following doctrines:

B—Biblical Authority

The Bible is the sole and final authority for all matters of faith and practice. *"All scripture is given by inspiration of God, and is profitable for doctrine, for reproof, for correction, for instruction in righteousness: That the man of God may be perfect* [mature, complete], *throughly furnished unto all good works"* (II Timothy 3:16, 17). God gave us the Bible; the Bible is the boss. The Bible is right, and man is wrong. If the Bible is right, let God be true and every man a liar (Romans 3:4).

A—The Autonomy of the Local Church

The word *autonomy* is not often used, but the word simply means "self-governing." The only people who make decisions in a Baptist church are the body of believers who are members of that church.

Every independent Baptist church should be self-governing (with no governing headquarters) and self-propagating (churches start churches).

P—The Priesthood of the Believers

I Timothy 2:5 says, *"For there is one God, and one mediator between God and men, the man Christ Jesus."* Only one person can intercede for you to God, and that Person is Jesus Christ, your Intercessor and your Mediator.

I Peter 2:5, *"Ye also, as lively stones, are built up a spiritual house, an holy priesthood, to offer up spiritual sacrifices, acceptable to God by Jesus Christ."* This verse says we are priests before God; we are a holy priesthood. We can go directly to God because we have Jesus Christ! Jesus is our priest, and you and I are members of the priesthood of the believers, which means that we have direct access to God. A Christian does not have to go through a pastor or a priest or a father to get to God. You can go right to God yourself through the person of Jesus Christ; you have access to Him.

T—TWO ORDINANCES

I Corinthians 11:1, 2, *"Be ye followers of me, even as I also am of Christ. Now I praise you, brethren, that ye remember me in all things, and keep the ordinances, as I delivered them to you."* The two ordinances that God gave the local church to perform are baptism and the Lord's Supper. Some religious organizations call these ordinances sacraments, but neither baptism nor the Lord's Supper are sacraments. A *sacrament* is "something that is needed additionally for salvation."

You do not have to get baptized to go to heaven. You do not have to take the Lord's Supper to go to heaven. These ordinances are part of the local church, administered by the local church. The local church also oversees the baptizing of a convert. A person does not have to be baptized by the pastor. Philip was one of the deacons in the early church in Acts chapter 8 who baptized the Ethiopian eunuch on his way to North Africa; he was a representative of his local church.

I—INDIVIDUAL SOUL LIBERTY

Romans 14:12, *"So then every one of us shall give account of himself to God."* The Baptists have always believed that salvation should not be coerced. If America's President announced that everyone had to be a Baptist, the people who would be the most vocal and adamantly against instituting a state religion would be the Baptists. Everyone has his own responsibility before God to believe or receive the Gospel.

Augustine of Hippo, who was probably the first Christian philosopher, understood that the Roman Empire was God's way of spreading and safeguarding the truths of Christianity throughout the known world. Augustine went so far as to say that the official religion would be Christianity, but making such a declaration was not a good idea. Becoming a Christian is an individual choice.

I cannot choose Christianity for my children; neither can you choose it for your children. We cannot choose Christianity for our mom, our dad, or our siblings. Everyone is individually responsible to accept Christ. A person's salvation should not be coerced, and every person is directly responsible to God for himself. Judging the motives of other people's hearts is not a biblical practice.

S—Saved and Baptized Church Membership

This particular tenet has probably gotten more Baptists into trouble than any other one and has caused more blood to be shed by Baptist people than any other. In order to be a member of a Baptist church, you must have a testimony of salvation, and you must be baptized after your salvation. Many religions will make you a member at birth, at baptism, or at a christening, but that is not what the Bible teaches. Not one baby was ever baptized in the Bible; babies were dedicated to the Lord by their parents. Neither baptism nor christening make a baby a member of the church. Based upon the Scripture, someone is baptized after he or she has believed. *"Then they that gladly received his word were baptized: and the same day there were added unto them about three thousand souls"* (Acts 2:41).

In years past and even today in some parts of the world, many Baptist people have faced bitter persecution whenever someone was baptized. Even the reformers, such as John Calvin, Zwingli, and Martin Luther were very frustrated by baptisms and, as a result, were very cruel. When these new believers came to the Baptist church, they would be asked, "When did you get baptized?" If the new convert answered, "When

I was a baby," they were informed that according to the Bible, they needed to be baptized again.

This being *re-baptized* frustrated those who saw their being baptized again after salvation as rejecting the church's baptism. The Baptists were not rejecting the baptism; they were rejecting the wrong way of baptizing. Being baptized is like wearing a wedding band. If a single person puts on a wedding band, he is not automatically married. The ring is a symbol to tell others that a man has made his vows to the person he loves, and she accepted him. By wearing a wedding ring, a husband is saying, "I am not ashamed of being associated with my wife; I am honored to wear my wedding band."

When someone gets baptized at a church service, he is identifying with Jesus and is showing others that he is not ashamed of the Saviour. Anyone who is saved should follow the Lord in believer's baptism.

The church is like a hospital that helps the sick and the grieving; the church encourages people through difficult times. Those who have lost loved ones have said to me, "Pastor, I don't know how unsaved people who don't have a church survive the loss. What a blessing to have somebody there to care for me, to love me, and to encourage me through my time of loss!" Those who attend a church should support the church, love the church, love what the church believes, propagate the gospel of Christ, and encourage their fellow members. Becoming a member of a local, New Testament, Bible-believing church is a responsibility and a privilege. I love pastoring a church, and I am grateful for the church.

T—Two Offices
Philippians 1:1 lists the two offices in a local church: the

pastor and deacons. The deacons help the pastor. The book of I Timothy lists their qualifications.

S—Separation of Church and State

The phrase "separation of church and state" initially was coined by the Baptists who were striving for religious toleration. Their leader was God—not the government. Everything in society and in an institution needs a leader. We wouldn't want to serve in a military where everybody from the general to the private had equal authority. The military is structured because of the need for an authority. A school with the students having equal authority with the teachers and the principal would be in chaos. Somebody has to be in charge. For instance, when a problem arises in a restaurant, a patron doesn't say, "Let me talk to the dish washer or the cook." Obviously, the person would ask to speak to the manager. You wouldn't want to eat at a restaurant where everyone had equal authority; a structure needs to be in place. We can fight God's authority structure, but quite frankly, our arms are too short to box with God. The best plan is simply to bow to His authority as our God.

God made the husband the head of the home—exactly like Christ is the head of this church. The pastor is not the head of the church; Jesus should be the head of the church.

God has determined the head of every man is Christ; the husband is the head of his wife. Children do better when a dad loves God and their mom and when their mother loves God and their dad. Though that is the best way for a child to be reared, unfortunately the best does not always happen. Sin complicates the home. Sometime death takes place, and a widow has to rear her children alone. Sometimes single dads are rearing the children alone because of the passing of their spouse. Divorce is also a factor in creating single parent homes. The security of children is directly related to the safety of the marriage, which is why the husband should be the physical and the spiritual leader of the home. Men must never surrender their spiritual leadership of their home.

Obviously, when a mom is a single parent, some challenges will arise, but God still has an authority structure in place. Every lady who is struggling with an unsaved husband or a husband who is not right with God should meditate on and memorize I Peter 3:1-6. Consider the following:

- "What am I supposed to do?"
- "What can I do?"
- "What does God want me to do in my situation?"

I am confident God has the answers for every situation.

I am blessed to be married to a very special lady who I believe is a better Christian than I am. However, my wife is not the head of the Wilkerson home. God has made me, as the husband, the head of our home, so I never want to surrender the spiritual leadership of our home. I am the one who is responsible to say, "Let's pray about that matter." I believe God wants me to be the one to say, "Let's go to church." "No, you will not dress that way. That will be fixed before we leave the house." "Let's gather round the Scriptures." "Pay attention in church." "What did you learn in the Sunday school lesson?" That responsibility belongs to me!

That principle is backed up in I Corinthians 11:3, which says, *"But I would have you know, that the head of every man is Christ; and the head of the woman is the man; and the head of Christ is God."*

Ephesians 5:23, *"For the husband is the head of the wife, even as Christ is the head of the church: and he is the saviour of the body."* In this verse, God is saying the body has a head. The head is not the boss or a dictator. The head merely makes decisions for an arm to move left or to lift up. The head tells the body to walk to the right. The head tells the mouth to speak words and the lungs to provide the air to speak the words. Everything the body does is orchestrated by the head.

Everything we do should be brought to His attention. We should ask ourselves, "What does Jesus want done?" Sadly, we don't always do a good job with weighing our choices and basing them on the Bible.

In a meeting not too long ago, someone said, "If we do this, we can make this certain person happy." I responded to that comment with something like, "Well, you know, it really doesn't matter what everybody else thinks. What does the Lord want? Because it's His church."

My friend, the same is true in a home. We should ask ourselves what the Lord would want in our home because He is the head. The husband is not supposed to be an ogre or a hard head who says, "It's my way or the highway." The husband is to be the loving leader of the home. My hand does not fight with my head; it is glad to cooperate. Likewise, a wife and the children need to cooperate with the head of the home.

Ephesians 5:22 says, *"Wives, submit yourselves unto your own husbands, as unto the Lord."* In considering this Scripture, we see that God addressed the submissive one before He addressed the leader. Ephesians 6:1, *"Children, obey your parents in the Lord: for this is right. Honour thy father and mother; (which is the first commandment with promise;) That it may be well with thee, and thou mayest live long on the earth."* Later in verse 4, God says, *"And, ye fathers, provoke not your children to wrath: but bring them up in the nurture and admonition of the Lord."* God addresses the employees and then the employers. I can only lead my wife in our home because she follows me. The only reason I can be the pastor of a church is that the people allow me. If the people won't follow me, then I will not be a pastor for very long.

Much of authority rests upon submission and yielding to the proper role. God places that responsibility on the follower. A wife is not responsible for the head of the house; that responsibility is on the husband. God knows how to correct the husband, but the wife's responsibility is to submit. The Bible says, *"Wives, submit yourselves unto your own husbands as unto the Lord...."* and *"Children obey your parents in the Lord for this is right"*—not because the parents are correct and not because the husband is right or is making the right decision or even a wise decision. Followers are to submit because the leader is in the place of the Lord. The Bible says that the head of every man is Christ, and the head of every woman is the man. We are to humbly follow God's model; men are to be the physical and spiritual head of the house.

5.
GIVE YOUR CHILD A GOOD NAME
AND HELP HIM KEEP IT GOOD.

M Y DAD WANTED us to have good names, so he gave his sons the names of the four Gospels: Matthew, Mark, Luke, John. I often kid that he should have named my sisters Acts and Romans; he named them Janna and Mary, which are also Bible names. He would oftentimes refer to the last name Wilkerson when we would attempt to argue, "Well, somebody else...."

Before we could finish, he would interrupt, "What's their last name?"

We would tell him the name, knowing what was coming next.

"Oh, so it's not Wilkerson? That name is a good name, and I want you to have a good name. When the Wilkerson name is spoken, people will automatically think honest or dishonest, late or on time, hardworking or lazy, kind or cruel, generous or stingy. Your mom and I have given you a good name. Work hard to keep that name what it should be."

Proverbs 22:1 says, *"A good name is rather to be chosen than great riches...."* If you have a choice between having a good name or a pile of money, the Bible says to choose the good name! With a good name, you will have many more opportunities for earning capacity, for blessings, and for eternal matters.

6.

REMIND YOUR CHILDREN THAT CHRISTIAN MEANS TO BE CHRISTLIKE.

B E CHRISTLIKE IN your conduct, in your choice of music, in your choice of reading materials, and in your dress.

> Matthew 5:14-17, *"Ye are the light of the world. A city that is set on an hill cannot be hid. Neither do men light a candle, and put it under a bushel, but on a candlestick; and it giveth light unto all that are in the house. Let your light so shine before men, that they may see your good works, and glorify your Father which is in heaven."*

What you listen to, how you dress, how you conduct yourself, how you treat your family, how you take care of your lawn, and how you take care of your property will give others an opinion of Jesus. People will have either a good opinion or a negative opinion based upon how Christians conduct themselves.

Christians need to be distinctively different. We live in a world that says, "It doesn't really matter what's on the outside. What really matters is what's on the inside." Contrary to popular opinion, both the inside and the outside do matter. Indeed, God does look on the inside. *"...Man looketh on the outward appearance, but the LORD looketh on the heart"* (I Samuel 16:7). Because man does look on the outward appearance, that part of our walk with God needs to be considered and adjusted as needed. You and I are a reflection of the Lord Jesus Christ. The Bible says in I Corinthians 10:31, *"Whether therefore ye eat, or drink, or whatsoever ye do, do all to the glory of God."* The word *glory* means "to give others a good opinion of." Giving glory to God isn't simply saying, "Glory to God." It's whenever someone looks at your life or mine and says, "That person gives me a good opinion of Jesus."

Some time ago, one of our neighbors called over the fence between our properties to get our attention. They are not people who have ever come to our church, but they have told me they weren't going to come. I walked over to him, and he said, "I had dinner with a friend who wants to go into the ministry. I told him the guy who lives next to me is unbelievable; he and his family are real Christians. I have known people who say they're Christians, but these guys are like really Christian people. John, if I brought them over to eat, would you talk to them and show them what you do?"

I replied, "Sure, I'll be glad to do that. We can even bring them over to our house."

"I want him to meet you because you guys are not just Christians in your talk; you're like real Christians in your walk. I told my friend you all even shovel my driveway when it snows and share meals with me, and I don't even know why you do that."

This conversation validates how important it is that we are a good testimony. People cannot see what's in another's heart; obviously, they can hear how he talks. They can see what we do, and they can see how we love. *"By this shall all men know that ye are my disciples, if ye have love one to another"* (John 13:35).

I love to hear visitors to our church say, "This is a big church, but I feel like there's a lot of love here." Every time I hear that statement, my heart is blessed. One man said, "I've never been to a church like this. This church is bigger than my hometown! You know what? It's like you've got some vibes going on here in this church." And we didn't even have a rock band! He said in parting, "I feel like your church is like a welcoming place." Exactly! Welcome is exactly how we want unsaved people to feel when they walk through our church doors. We want them to be open to hear God's Word and to feel God's love. Since people cannot see our heart, that love and acceptance has to be shown on the outside. *"Let your light so shine before men."*

I Peter 2:9, *"But ye are a chosen generation, a royal priesthood, an holy nation, a peculiar people...."* That word *peculiar* doesn't mean "weird"; that word means "purchased." In other words, God has procured you; He has purchased you. You are not owned by yourself but by Someone else.

> *"That ye should shew forth the praises of him who hath called you out of darkness into his marvellous light. Which in time past were not a people, but are now the people of God: which had not obtained mercy, but now have obtained mercy. Dearly beloved, I beseech you as strangers and pilgrims..."* (I Peter 2:10, 11).

Since this world is not our home, we should abstain from fleshly lusts and desires. We need to take on a pilgrim mentality and not get caught up with the affairs of this world. The world is very attractive. Have you ever noticed how easy learning a rock song can be but how hard learning a memory verse or meditating on the Scriptures can be? For this reason, we must carefully guard our children and what goes in their eye gates and ear gates. Acts 4:20 says, *"For we cannot but speak the things which we have seen and heard."*

I Peter 2:12 continues, *"Having your conversation* [the way we live] *honest among the Gentiles* [the unsaved]: *that, where-as they speak against you as evildoers, they may by your good works, which they shall behold, glorify God in the day of visita-tion* [the day they hear the Gospel and judgment time]." The unsaved will remember you by your good works and what they saw in you: the way you dressed, the way you conducted your-self, the good deeds you did, and the honesty with which you handled your affairs. Your actions will glorify God when God visits the unsaved either in salvation or in judgment.

What goes on on the outside is very important; don't fool yourself. We are a chosen generation, a royal priesthood, a holy nation, and we should show forth the praise of God who called us out of darkness into His marvelous light (I Peter 2:9).

CHURCH ATTENDANCE AND BEHAVIOR

Don't ever come to church without coming as though it were the first time, as though it could be the best time, and as though it could be the last time.

– Vance Havner

1.
KEEP YOUR FAMILY IN EVERY CHURCH SERVICE AND ANY OTHER TIMES THE DOORS ARE OPEN.

W HEN A PREACHER was at a conference or revival during the week, my dad took the family to hear the preaching of God's Word. Because my dad did, I had the opportunity to hear Jack Hyles, Lester Roloff, John R. Rice, Harold Sightler, Tom Malone, Curtis Hutson, Myron Cedarholm, and many great preachers who are now in the presence of the Lord.

The first time I heard Bro. Hyles was as a nine-year-old. As a teen, I remember his preaching a sermon titled, "Let's Hear It for the Other Son," which addressed the story of the prodigal son. He said most people talk about the prodigal son's coming home, but that night he spoke of being proud of the son who stayed at home and didn't go out into sin. That sermon has remained fixed in my mind. I only had the privilege of hearing that sermon because my dad felt his children should be in church when preaching was taking place. My father believed in Romans 10:17, which says, *"So then faith cometh by hearing, and hearing by the word of God."* Because faith is generated as people hear the Word of God preached, young people need to hear God's Word preached.

We live in a day when people do not want to hear sound doctrine; they simply want to have someone tickle their ears and tell them to feel good about themselves. I Corinthians 1:18 says, *"For the preaching of the cross is to them that perish foolishness; but unto us which are saved it is the power of God."* The power of God happens in preaching. God has wisely chosen the foolishness of preaching to provide opportunities to come to know Christ.

Preaching is not in a pulpit alone; it is proclaiming God's truth. In fact, when a person goes soul winning, he is preaching because he is proclaiming God's truth to somebody. Christians can always have confidence in the power of the Gospel of Christ. Sometimes as I witness to people, I think they will not want to listen. Regardless of their background, giving them the Gospel will affect them because it's the dynamite of God that blows up in their hearts.

I once had the joy of leading a man to Christ who served in the Navy and was stationed at Great Lakes Naval Base. As I began to talk to him about the Lord, he shared the following story with me:

You know, I really am quite surprised that I'm even interested in what you have to say. Two years ago I wouldn't even have cared about what you had to say. I wouldn't have even let you open the Bible in my presence. My job in the military was to take bombs apart so they could be detonated safely. When I went home, I began showing my brother how to make a bomb, and it malfunctioned and blew up. I felt a piece of brass fly over my right ear and another over my head. I was a little shaken by the unexpected explosion. Then I looked at my brother, only to see him bent over in agony.

"I need help," he gasped and slumped to the floor.

Then I saw what another shard of metal had done

to his abdominal area. My brother began to beg, "Don't let me die! Don't let me die!"

This young man continued, "I was so traumatized by what I had caused, but now I realize how that trauma has caused me to listen to you today. I want to get saved."

How wonderful is the power of the Gospel! God's timing and our going are how people can hear the Word of God. I Corinthians 1:21, *"For after that in the wisdom of God the world by wisdom knew not God, it pleased God by the foolishness of preaching to save them that believe."*

Verse 27 continues, *"But God hath chosen the foolish things of the world to confound the wise; and God hath chosen the weak things of the world to confound the things which are mighty."* Parents need to get their children under the influence of the preaching of the Word of God. Everyone will be helped by the preaching of the Gospel.

I have shared the Gospel publicly with people who have become so angry. One time a lady got so angry with me that she threw a fit. I wasn't even talking to her; I was talking to someone else! She kept making disparaging noises of disapproval. I was thinking, *Why are you so upset?* She thought what I was sharing was foolishness, but for those of us who know Jesus Christ, we know it is the power of God!

My dad believed hearing the Word of God was vital and desperately needed. He made sure his children were in church when the doors were open.

2.

DON'T ALLOW YOUR CHILDREN TO PLAY, RUN, WRITE NOTES, EAT, CHEW GUM, OR TALK IN CHURCH.

THE BIBLE SAYS in Nehemiah 8 that whenever God's people gathered together, all the men, the women, and the children—who could understand—attended. They stood for hours as a family, listening to the Bible.

Parents of today are so easy on their kids. Many of the kids sitting in pews disfigure or tear up the bulletins or offering envelopes, goof around, chew gum, and snack during church time.

I can promise that my dad wasn't that permissive! I have seen enough kids to know that some preschoolers know how to behave themselves in church. If they don't, it's not the kids' fault; it's the parents' fault.

3.

DON'T LET YOUR CHILDREN SIT IN CHURCH WHEN THEY SHOULD BE STANDING.

DAD WOULD LOOK down the row to make sure everybody was standing. After we were seated, he would look down the aisle to make sure we weren't writing notes to each other, coloring pictures, or chewing gum. When it was time to stand and sing, he wouldn't let us sit down. At the appropriate times, we were to participate in the service.

In Nehemiah 8, after the building of the wall, Ezra called a meeting. The people built a pulpit from which the Book of the Law was to be read. When the Bible was read, everyone who had understanding of the spoken Word, including children, stood for at least a couple hours.

My dad shared that account with all of us and expected the same attention from his children because paying attention in church was a matter of importance to him. What my dad shared with me about paying attention in church, I have tried to share with my own children.

4.
WEAR THE BEST YOU HAVE TO CHURCH TO HONOR THE LORD.

I AM THANKFUL for learning this principle from my dad. When he would oftentimes make this statement on a Sunday afternoon, we would sometimes protest, "But, Dad, the other teenagers don't wear a tie on Sunday night."

He would always answer, "What's your last name, son? Do you like living here?"

"Umm, yes, sir."

"Then put on a tie," he would order.

Why would you wear your best? Today's society says, "Come as you are, and leave as you came. We'll pat you on the head, and we'll make you feel good about yourself." I don't think most people would attend a memorial service or a wedding wearing ripped or torn blue jeans and a T-shirt. When a person dresses appropriately, he gives respect to the people that he honors with his presence.

People do not attend church to honor the pastor; rather, they come to honor the Lord Jesus Christ. Church is not a fashion show for people.

I Corinthians 10:31-33 teaches,

"Whether therefore ye eat, or drink, or whatsoever ye do, do all to the glory of God. ³²Give none offence, neither to the Jews, nor to the Gentiles, nor to the church of

God: ³³*Even as I please all men in all things, not seeking mine own profit, but the profit of many, that they may be saved."*

A Christian's dress should always be God-honoring; thus, I believe a Christian should always consider wearing his best to church services.

5.
KEEP YOUR CHILDREN IN CHURCH AND IN THE WORD OF GOD.

HEBREWS 10:25 SAYS, *"Not forsaking the assembling of ourselves together as the manner of some is; but exhorting one another: and so much the more, as ye see the day approaching."*

Make church a priority! I Timothy 4:16 says, *"Take heed unto thyself, and unto the doctrine; continue in them: for in doing this thou shalt both save thyself, and them that hear thee."*

When I was a teenager, my family of eight lived in an old farmhouse in the middle of nowhere, with four rooms and a bathroom attached to the side of the house. My two sisters slept in the living room near the Ben Franklin stove. All four of us boys slept in one bed in one bedroom, and my parents had the other bedroom. The fourth room was a kitchen. One Saturday night our area had a bad snowstorm that continued into Sunday morning. I remember getting up, looking out the door, seeing the heavy snowfall. and informing my dad. Dad looked out the window and said, "We're still going to church."

We all protested. "Dad! There's too much snow. We'll get stuck. We won't even make it to the end of the drive to the gravel road!"

Dad looked at us and declared, "We're Wilkersons. We don't miss church. We're going to try."

We had a 1972 Buick Electra that was built like a boat.

I remember Dad's gunning that car down a hill in order to make it up the next. When he hit the gully at the bottom, the car came to a dead stop. Dad ordered, "John, Matt, Mark, and Luke, get out and push."

We all immediately protested, "Dad, this is nuts!"

I added, "We've got our church clothes on!"

"Get out and push, John!"

I got out with my brothers, and we pushed and rocked the car back and forth over and over again. Finally he said, "All right, guys, forget it. Let's go home."

We all trudged back to the house and sat in the living room as Dad announced, "All right, since we cannot go to church, we're going to have church here. John, get ready to lead the singing. Matthew, you give the announcements. Mark, you're going to preach the message. Luke, you're taking the offering. Janna and Mary, you're singing the special." Dad assigned everyone a certain responsibility, and a regular church service was held in the farmhouse that morning. Truly, that snowfall is the only time that I ever remember missing church. I well remember that Sunday morning when I said to my dad, "I don't think we're going to make it to the gravel road."

My family's church was more than fifteen miles away; however, we were always there—even before the janitor arrived most of the time. My dad volunteered his kids to clean the church every Saturday. I have personally vacuumed auditoriums hundreds of times. I have cleaned bathrooms, mowed lawns, shoveled snow, and swept sidewalks, which is what my dad wanted us to do. I didn't like being "volunteered" back then, but I am thankful today.

When the family traveled on vacation, we always attended a church. I always voted for "Roadside Baptist Church" or "Rest

Stop Baptist Church," but not Dad. Before cell phones were even a dream, we would stop at a gas station and go through the yellow pages of the phone book to find a church. Dad always insisted on an independent, fundamental, Baptist church that held Sunday morning, Sunday night, and midweek services. We would then stop, maybe at a truck stop a mile or two away, change into our church clothes, and find the church. We would arrive early if we could.

Of those times, I used to think, *My dad's a nut; he's crazy!* Our big family was always noticeable, and we frequently heard the question, "Does your family sing?"

We kids would answer, "No, we don't sing. Thank you very much."

But Dad would interrupt, "Yes, they do. They'll sing."

We would protest, "Dad, please. You're killing us."

He would then choose a song for us to sing and say, "Get up there."

We would continue to protest, "No, Dad! We don't even know these people."

"God will use you! Get up there; let's go." Dad's goal was to keep us in church and to keep us serving in church.

My dad was always faithful to Sunday school and church. He also made sure his children were in Sunday school and church. We all sat together, listened to the preaching, and sang the songs. We all used a songbook. Either we had our own songbook or shared with someone. We weren't allowed to stand and not participate while waiting for the song to conclude. If we didn't sing, we would be meeting my dad afterward for a little "powwow," and as I sometimes jokingly say, "He would do the 'powing,' and we would do the 'wowing.' "

To my dad, church was important, and the Scriptures

were important. We weren't allowed to set anything on our Bible. Tossing our Bible brought all kinds of trouble for us. He taught us to make much of the Bible. He always liked for us to be memorizing verses. Hearing him ask, "What verse are you memorizing?" was not uncommon.

We would tell him what verse we were working on because my dad simply would not settle for our not learning and memorizing the Scriptures.

THE SCRIPTURES

Do not have your concert first, and then tune your instrument afterward. Begin the day with the Word of God and prayer, and get first of all into harmony with Him.

– Hudson Taylor

1.
THE BIBLE SHOULD BE YOUR CHILD'S MOST IMPORTANT BOOK.

DON'T ALLOW DUST to accumulate on the Bible or allow children to carelessly throw the Bible around. God places a great emphasis on the Scriptures. All but two verses of Psalm 119, which is the longest chapter in the Bible, directly reference the Word of God. Though I do not like to admit this, I go through frequent seasons of time where reading the Word of God can become laborious, and I even find the Bible is not quite as sweet to me as it should be.

Several years ago someone gave me the idea to read a section of eight verses of Psalm 119 every night prior to going to bed. I can promise that reading only eight verses that reference the importance of the Bible will warm the cool heart.

Many familiar verses can be found in this Psalm:

"*Blessed are the undefiled in the way, who walk in the law of the LORD*" (verse 1).

"*Wherewithal shall a young man cleanse his way? by taking heed thereto according to thy word*" (verse 9).

"*Thy word have I hid in mine heart, that I might not sin against thee*" (verse 11).

"*It is good for me that I have been afflicted; that I might learn thy statutes*" (verse 71).

"*For ever, O LORD, thy word is settled in heaven*" (verse 89).

"O how I love thy law! it is my meditation all the day" (verse 97).

"Thy word is a lamp unto my feet, and a light unto my path" (verse 105).

"Great peace have they which love thy law: and nothing shall offend them" (verse 165).

As I fell asleep, I would be thinking about one of those verses, and the end result of my giving attention to Psalm 119 was a renewed love for the Bible.

My dad would try to make sure that we had our Bibles. Children tend to be forgetful and leave their Bibles in Sunday school classes or in the car. He was very particular about our making sure we put our Bibles away in a safe place. We were not allowed to throw them around or put anything else on top of our Bibles. He wanted us to treasure the Word of God.

He would often quiz, "What's the Bible?" and we would answer, "The Bible's the Word of God." My father always made much of the Scriptures.

2.
USE THE KING JAMES VERSION
OF THE BIBLE.

PSALM 12:6, 7, SAYS, *"The words of the LORD are pure words: as silver tried in a furnace of earth, purified seven times. Thou shalt keep them, O LORD, thou shalt preserve them from this generation for ever."* The words of God are eternal. The Bible is a Book that God has chosen to preserve.

Baptists have historically believed the King James Version of the Bible to be God's preserved, inspired Word for English-speaking people. If you have difficulty with understanding the words, the Defined King James Bible, published by The Bible for Today Press, Collingswood, New Jersey, would be a consideration for you. The unfamiliar words are defined throughout this Bible. If you have a choice between Coca-Cola and a generic brand, which one would you want to drink? I doubt you would want a cheap imitation of the real thing. If you want the real thing and if money is not an option, you would go for the real thing. No one wants a cheap imitation of the real thing.

The same is true for our Bible. In many translations, Acts 8:37 has been omitted. The translators have omitted fasting and the blood of Christ in some places. Some versions even say that Mary was a "young woman"—not a virgin. People tend to accept the differences without finding out the problems. I'm so grateful my dad reminded me, "Son, just stay with the King James Version of the Bible."

The proof is in the product. People who stray away from the King James Version of the Bible often soften their stance on biblical holiness and separation. I am certainly not saying that everyone who has a King James Bible is holy. What I am saying is that the King James Bible has what I believe to be a purity in its pages.

Years ago our church in Long Beach, California, had a ministry to the homeless called the Eagles Ministry. A young man named Geronimo and his girlfriend, Jessica, who were staying at a park in downtown Long Beach, came to the service. Geronimo settled his salvation, and Jessica got saved. Both were baptized, and they began attending every service as a result of this ministry. When they returned the next week, I greeted them by calling them by name, and Geronimo said, "I can't believe how the people care for us. We love it here."

They continued to stay in the park in Long Beach, living off the benevolence of people. The day finally came when Geronimo said, "Pastor, you know what? I have never been bothered about Jessica and me living together. But I feel like we should get married. My folks didn't even get married. How does someone get married? I don't even know how to do it. What do you do?"

I was thrilled to say the least! "Well, Geronimo, you have to get a marriage certificate. Let's counsel some and plan it out."

"How much does it cost?"

"Well, a marriage certificate costs about $75, so we'll help you with that fee. But first, I want to talk to you and make sure you marry in the Lord's will. Then I can help you with that marriage certificate."

"No, Pastor. We'll work on it."

They collected aluminum cans and sold them, and Geronimo worked at a few jobs. Sure enough, they came back about five days later and said, "Here's our marriage certificate. What do we do now?"

I counseled with them, and about a month from the day they were saved, they got married on a Sunday afternoon. Dr. David Gibbs was preaching that Sunday night, and they sat together in the service—still dressed in their wedding attire. Dr. Gibbs said, "I've preached thousands of times, but I have never preached to someone who just got married and attended a preaching service in wedding attire." We helped them have a beautiful little get-away for a honeymoon.

When the newlyweds returned, they worked on finding a place to stay, and they both found jobs. One day Geronimo came to my office to tell me the police had issued a warrant for his arrest. He had gotten involved in a check-cashing fraud. Geronimo didn't want to go back to jail with all the blessed changes in his new life in Christ. "Pastor, what do you think I ought to do?"

"Geronimo, I'll go to court with you. Let's see what the Lord will do for you."

I had watched him become a contributing member of society. I was so disappointed when the judge sentenced him to over a year in jail. In spite of the setback, the Lord helped him and his wife. Jessica acquired a very lucrative job working with staffing nurses all over California. I stayed in touch with Geronimo when he was in prison. He read his Bible through one time, and his New Testament through 30 times while he was in jail. He returned to church like a walking Bible and continued growing. One day he knocked on my office door and said, "Pastor, I think God's calling me to preach."

I shared this story of Geronimo and Jessica for one reason:

before he went to jail, I gave him a King James Bible, and I shared the same truths with him that are in this chapter. When he went into prison, he managed to get a paperback King James Bible. He read it daily and marked it up. The chaplain noticed how hungry he was for the Word of God and offered him a brand-new NIV leather Bible. "Obviously, you have a real heart for the Lord," he commented.

Geronimo thought, "Pastor taught me that I should only read the KJV, but Pastor doesn't know everything. It can't be any big deal." When the chaplain brought him the NIV Bible, Geronimo gave his worn, paperback King James Bible to another Christian. Geronimo said he started reading the NIV, and after four days, he realized he wasn't getting the same spiritual substance from his reading, but he didn't want to give up his beautiful, brand-new leather Bible that smelled and looked so good. He read it another day, and he said, "Finally, Pastor, it was all I could take. I saw the guy who had my old Bible in the yard, and said, "Hey, can I swap with you? You can have this real nice Bible. He was very happy to return my old Bible." Geronimo used that paperback Bible during the months he was there. He saw the reality of the cheap imitation versus the real thing. He realized he wasn't growing the same with another translation. Geronimo is now pastoring a church and serving the Lord. He has a sweet family with a beautiful testimony.

How very glad I am that God gave me a dad who told me to stay with the King James Bible!

3.

TEACH YOUR CHILDREN THAT HELL IS REAL, CREATION IS TRUE, MAN'S SINFUL NATURE IS BAD, AND OTHER BASIC BIBLE DOCTRINES.

W E CURRENTLY LIVE in a society where people no longer want to believe that hell is real. They think that *hell* is merely a curse word, but contrary to popular opinion, hell is a real place, and people will stay there until they're taken out for the great white throne judgment and cast into the lake of fire. If the concept that hell is a real place could resonate into my heart, I think I would be a better soul winner. The founder and editor of *The Sword of the Lord*, Dr. John R. Rice, said, "What a compelling motive we have for prayer, for preaching, for soul winning when we learn that every responsible human being who leaves this world without a definite change in heart immediately lifts his eyes in Hell, tormented in flame!" I believe if this concept could resonate in your heart, you'd be a better soul winner too.

Teach your kids that creation is true. We live in a world that teaches that evolution is true. Evolution is nothing more than a fairy tale with millions and millions of years as its magic wand. What is real is that creation is true. God's creation of the world is described in the book of Genesis.

Man's sinful human nature is bad innately. Not a man on

earth "...*doeth good, no, not one*" (Romans 3:12). "*The heart is deceitful above all things, and desperately wicked: who can know it?*" (Jeremiah 17:9).

One time a man told me, "If you say that verse one more time, I'm never coming back to church again! My heart is not desperately wicked; I've been cleansed by the blood of Jesus."

Man's heart is deceitful, and the person who trusts in his own heart is a fool. How I think, how I feel, and what I want are very deceptive, and that's why we need to turn to the Scriptures for the basic doctrines of the Bible. II Timothy 2:15, "*Study to shew thyself approved unto God, a workman that needeth not to be ashamed, rightly dividing the word of truth.*"

Doctrine determines destiny; what you believe determines how you behave. Long before there's a shipwreck doctrinally, there's a swerve in position (I Timothy 1:6, 19).

4.

TEACH THEM NOT TO BELIEVE EVERYTHING THEY HEAR OR ARE TAUGHT BUT TO TEST EVERYTHING WITH THE SCRIPTURES.

M Y DAD WOULD say, "Kids, don't accept everything people say. You need to evaluate it based upon what the Bible says." Doing so requires skill, discernment, and wisdom. I have heard men of God make statements that do not "hit me quite right." I don't think it is disrespectful to consider, "Is that what the Bible says?" Colossians 2:8 says, *"Beware lest any man spoil you through philosophy and vain deceit, after the tradition of men, after the rudiments of the world, and not after Christ."* We need to evaluate everything through the sieve of what the Bible says and realize that traditions, rudiments of the world, and philosophies can lead us astray. *Philosophies* are "sets of values that govern your decisions."

In Acts 17, the Apostle Paul had been in the city of Thessalonica. From there he fled to Berea where he made an observation that God chose to include in the Scripture.

> Acts 17:10, 11, *"And the brethren immediately sent away Paul and Silas by night unto Berea: who coming thither went into the synagogue of the Jews. [11]These were more noble than those in Thessalonica, in that they received the word with all readiness of mind, and searched the scriptures daily, whether those things were so."*

Why were the Bereans more noble than the people of Thessalonica? They received the Word with all readiness of mind.

You are noble when you pay attention and listen in church and receive the Word of God. Receiving the Word of God is not where nobility ends though. The Bereans not only received the Word of God with readiness of mind, but they searched the Scriptures daily to see whether those things were so. They evaluated! They searched the Scriptures to be sure what Paul said was true. I don't mind when church members search the Scriptures for support for what I preach. If I say something that disagrees with the Bible, the Bible is right, and I am wrong! If something is my opinion, I need to be very careful to say, "This is my opinion; it's not necessarily what the Bible says."

If you hear something that seems to disagree with the Bible, go with the Bible! Searching the Word of God for truth is a discipline each Christian needs in his life. How I thank God for my father's helping me with understanding that I cannot believe everything I hear or everything I am taught. We must carefully evaluate everything through the sieve and the filter of God's Word.

5.

PERSONALLY STAY IN THE
WORD OF GOD
AND IN AN ATTITUDE OF PRAYER.

JOSHUA 1:8 SAYS, *"This book of the law shall not depart out of thy mouth; but thou shalt meditate therein day and night, that thou mayest observe to do according to all that is written therein: for then thou shalt make thy way prosperous, and then thou shalt have good success."* This verse is the only place in the Bible where the word *success* is mentioned. In this case, success revolves around what I do with the Bible. One of my teachers in college once said, "What you do with the Bible determines what God does with you." Such admonition reminds us to make much of the Scriptures.

Parents, we cannot possibly reproduce in our children what we don't have. If we do not love the Bible, we will struggle to rear children who love the Bible. We must have the Word in our heart. The book of Deuteronomy is a book of remembrance. God wants us to remember. The people whom God was addressing did not cross the Red Sea as adults. They were almost all under 40 years of age, and God wanted to remind them of some things.

Deuteronomy 6:4-7, *"Hear, O Israel: The LORD our God is one LORD: ⁵And thou shalt love the LORD thy God with all thine heart, and with all thy soul, and with all thy might. ⁶And these words, which I command thee this day, shall be in thine heart: ⁷And thou shalt teach them diligently unto thy children, and shalt talk of them when thou sittest in thine house, and when thou walkest by the way, and when thou liest down, and when thou risest up."*

God was reminding His people that, first of all, they needed to have God's Word in them, and secondly, they needed to pass that on to their children. When should they teach the Word to their children? When they go to bed at night, when they wake up in the morning, when they walk by the way, and at every opportunity. God wants parents to look for times to pass on the Scriptures to their children.

Then we are to be people of prayer. Luke 18:1 says, *"...men ought always to pray, and not to faint."* Stay faithful to praying without ceasing.

I always loved the times my dad said, "John, I'm praying for you." Sometimes he would say, "I prayed several times for you last night." I am glad that my dad made prayer real to me.

Sometimes he would say, "When I couldn't sleep last night, I just kept praying for you kids. I prayed for you, I prayed for Matt, I prayed for Mark, I prayed for Luke, I prayed for Janna and for Mary." I now try to do the same for my own children.

Grandpa and Grandma, tell your kids and your grandkids that you prayed for them. Pray that God would strengthen them with His might in the inner man. Pray that they would be strong in the inner man. Say often to your children, "I'm praying for you."

Text your children a message that you are praying for them. When our oldest son was in college, oftentimes I would pray for him, and later I would text him to say, "Hey, I prayed for you. I love you. I'm proud of you. Keep living for the Lord." Inevitably he always texted back to say, "Thanks, Dad; I appreciate it."

Your children need to know you love them enough to pray for them. Knowing that someone is praying for us is very important to know.

PRAYER

In prayer it
is better to have
a heart without words
than words without a heart.

– John Bunyan

1.
TEACH YOUR CHILDREN TO PRAY FOR AND TO HELP OTHERS.

M Y DAD WAS extremely sensitive to the underdog when it came to helping people. One time when I was fifteen years old, I said, "Dad, I'm so bored."

"I'm so sorry to hear that. I'll fix that situation for you."

"Dad, what are you talking about?"

He called four widows in our church, and before I knew what was happening, I was no longer bored because I was busy washing windows, cleaning gutters, pulling weeds, and performing any other chore those ladies needed—all because "My son just wanted to show he loves the Lord" or so my dad kindly explained to them. You know, I can promise you that I never again made the mistake of saying, "I'm bored" to my father. I can promise that my father fixed my boredom very quickly.

Dad later explained, "Bored people are boring, and I'm going to fix that with you, John." For several weeks, I was quite busy with no pay. If there was any pay involved, my dad must have collected because he didn't share with me. If the word *bored* was mentioned in my dad's presence, he would say, "Find someone to help. Pray for others and help others."

Dr. Hyles frequently quoted the poem *Others* by Charles D. Meigs from the pulpit.

> *Lord, help me* live from day to day
> In such a self-forgetful way

That even when I kneel to pray
My prayer shall be for others.

Refrain:
Yes, others, Lord, yes, others,
Let this my motto be;
Help me to live for others,
That I may live like Thee.

Help me in all the work I do
To ever be sincere and true,
And know that all I'd do for You
Must needs be done for others.

Let "Self" be crucified and slain
And buried deep: and all in vain
May efforts be to rise again,
Except to live for others.

So when my work on earth is done,
And my new work in heav'n's begun,
I'll praise You for the crown I've won,
But praise You more for others.

I'm thankful that my dad passed on to all of his children an attitude of trying to help other people. We aren't always successful in our efforts, and we haven't always helped others wisely, but if my siblings and I do help other people, it's primarily because our father consistently taught us to pray and to help other people. Philippians 2:4 says, *"Look not every man on his own things, but every man also on the things of others."*

I Thessalonians 5:25 directs, *"Brethren, pray for us."*

2.
TEACH YOUR CHILDREN TO PRAY FOR OTHERS FIRST AND THEN THEMSELVES.

TEACHING CHILDREN TO pray for others first and then for their own needs is an attitude that needs to be cultivated. Because all humans are naturally selfish, they think about "number 1" (themselves) with regularity. When they pray, they very often pray prominently for their own needs.

I remember hearing my dad tell us, "You've got to pray for other people." Philippians 2:4, *"Look not every man on his own things, but every man also on the things of others."* We can become so consumed with our own needs that we forget others' needs, but the Bible teaches us to look at the needs of others.

I Timothy 2:1, 2, *"I exhort therefore, that, first of all, supplications, prayers, intercessions, and giving of thanks, be made for all men; ²For kings, and for all that are in authority; that we may lead a quiet and peaceable life in all godliness and honesty."* When we pray for others, we should include our government leaders and officials. We should pray for our President regardless of his political views. I keep a picture of the first family in my Bible and exchange that picture when there is a new President. On the back of that picture, I have written the names of other elected officials as a reminder to me to pray for our government leaders. We should pray for our mayor and city officials. We should pray for the governor of our state.

We need to ask the Lord to help them simply because no

one can quite complicate our lives like the government can. If anyone in government ever does complicate your life, you will be able to say, "I've been praying for you." We should desire to live out our Christianity with quietness, honesty, and sincerity. As we do so, we should pray for our government leaders.

I Timothy 2:3, 4, *"For this is good and acceptable in the sight of God our Saviour; ⁴Who will have all men to be saved, and to come unto the knowledge of the truth."* God also wants us to pray for the salvation of souls. Are we praying for unsaved people in our sphere of influence—our neighbors, our friends, our coworkers? Prayer will change those who come to Christ.

Prayer changes one's perspective. When I see my friends, I think about whether or not they are saved, and I ask God to save them. When I see my neighbors across the fence, I pray for them. I don't know how much my intercession brings the gospel of Christ to them, but I do know prayer makes me more sensitive to get the gospel to my neighbors. Pray for the unsaved.

Praying for other people's needs and then your own is the biblical way. Jesus didn't come to be ministered to; He came to minister (Matthew 20:26). *"Who, being in the form of God, thought it not robbery to be equal with God: But made himself of no reputation, and took upon him the form of a servant, and was made in the likeness of men"* (Philippians 2:6, 7). Think of others and pray for others.

Hebrews 7:25, *"Wherefore he is able also to save them to the uttermost that come unto God by him, seeing he ever liveth to make intercession for them."* This verse is saying that Jesus is able to save anyone—to the uttermost and from the guttermost. He can save anybody because *he ever liveth*, which means He's alive forever. Right now, Jesus is making intercession for man. Praying for other people is a Christlike characteristic.

3.
PRAY FOR YOUR CHILDREN EVERY TIME THEY COME TO MIND.

JAMES 5:16 SAYS, "...*the effectual fervent prayer of a righteous man availeth much.*" Parents, let me encourage you to pray for your children.

When my family would drive through the night and while everyone was asleep, Dad would later say, "I just prayed for you all night."

I know for sure that my dad probably prayed me out of some very tempting situations. I have never had alcohol to my mouth although I wanted to see what it was like to take a drink. Though I wanted to smoke, I have never smoked a cigarette. Because I was curious, several times I allowed myself to be put into positions where it was just me, the Devil, and God. I had a curiosity for sin even though I was reared in a sheltered environment. I am so thankful I had a dad and a mom who consistently prayed for me.

Have you ever been driving somewhere and the face of a loved one crossed your mind? Why do people come to your mind? Maybe the Holy Spirit was reminding you to pray for the loved one at that time. Each of us should pray for our loved ones and our children by name. As you call their names out before the Lord, pray that God would help them. Pray for their future spouses. Grandparents, pray for your grandchildren. Every time God brings them to your mind, pray for them.

By the way, God didn't call us to worry, which is taking on responsibility God never intended for us to have. God didn't call for us to be fearful. God did not give us the spirit of fear, but He did call us to pray!

STRIVE TO ALWAYS BE IN AN ATTITUDE OF PRAYER.

I Thessalonians 5:17 says, *"Pray without ceasing."* My dad was extremely good at living this verse. I know he prayed a lot, and I'm grateful for the many hours he would spend in prayer.

Whenever the Lord brings a specific matter to mind, pray. *"Men ought always to pray, and not to faint"* (Luke 18:16). Have an attitude of prayer.

4.
WHEN TAKING A TRIP, ASK THE CHILDREN TO PRAY FOR SAFETY.

WHEN OUR FAMILY took a trip anywhere, my dad would rarely pray in the driver's seat. He would generally ask one of us boys to pray or even one of our sisters to pray before leaving. He would say, "Before we leave, let's one of us pray. John, you pray this time" or "Matt, you pray this time."

He would encourage us to pray publicly in front of our family. Even as a teenager, I felt like remembering to pray was a great testimony. Of course, that principle can be found all throughout the Bible:

"...*Men ought always to pray, and not to faint*" (Luke 18:1).

"*Pray without ceasing*" (I Thessalonians 5:17).

These are only two of the verses that continually remind Christians to talk to the Lord. When getting in the car to go someplace, how much simpler can it be than to say, "Why don't we pray before leaving, and John, you pray for us"?

I am still so thankful for that training by my father.

FAMILY
COMMUNICATION

Family Rules:
1. Put the other person first.
2. Speak with love.
3. Tell the truth.
4. Mind your manners.
5. Make the right choice.
6. Guard your heart.
7. Always do your best.
8. Be courageous.
9. Forgive freely.
10. Be thankful.

INTRODUCTION

Deuteronomy 6:6, 7, *"And these words, which I command thee this day, shall be in thine heart: ⁷And thou shalt teach them diligently unto thy children, and shalt talk of them when thou sittest in thine house, and when thou walkest by the way, and when thou liest down, and when thou risest up."*

THESE TWO VERSES contain admonition from Moses to the children of God—most of whom did not cross the Red Sea unless they were babes in the arms of their parents. Most were now young people. Those forty years old and older had died in the wilderness, but before this new generation of Israelites crossed the Jordan River into the Promised Land, Moses reminded them of their responsibilities from the book of Deuteronomy.

This Scripture teaches that for parents to rear and train their children correctly, parents must have a relationship with the Lord built on having His Word in their hearts. This Scripture teaches that parents need to diligently teach their children—every child, all the time, and in every place. When we lie down and when we wake up, we need to always be in the teaching mode.

Parents, we need to use every available opportunity to teach our children the truths of God's Word and His ways.

1.
IN FAMILY MATTERS,
SPEAK TO YOUR CHILDREN AS ADULTS.

I OFTEN HEARD my dad say, "I want to treat you like an adult." This point leads me to stress the importance of reaching the heart of the oldest child. Certainly all of your children are important, but the oldest needs a tremendous amount of attention. The firstborn especially needs to have a great amount of influence on him early because that child passes on what he has learned to his siblings. My dad would oftentimes say to me, "Son, I want to talk to you like an adult," and he would quote I Timothy 4:12, *"Let no man despise thy youth; but be thou an example of the believers."* When family matters arose that needed to be addressed, he would not talk to us like little kids; he would engage us as adults in conversation.

Dad also expected his children to sit in church like adults. I remember when I was in fourth grade, my dad instructed me to sit in a folding chair on the second row at a Sword of the Lord Conference and added, "You stay there until the service is over." Dr. Jack Hyles and Dr. John R. Rice were both preaching that night. He made sure I had already gone to the bathroom so I wouldn't leave in the middle of the service. I sat and listened to two preachers preach after the congregation sang several songs, but I did not leave my seat.

2.
CHILDREN NEED A MOTHER
WHO WILL LISTEN AND LOVE THEM.

A LONG WITH A listening and loving mother, children also need "a loud-mouthed dad" at times—my father's exact wording. The synergy of a husband and a wife together working with their children is so vital and important. Someone said, "Our children's security will be based on the relationship of their mom and dad."

I remember lying in bed as a fourth grader, at a time when my dad was going through a tense period of pressure in his life. That tenseness spilled over into our home and my parents' marriage. I remember hearing my parents in a harsh conversation, and I was scared. I was only nine years old, and I overheard these words: "If it weren't for the kids, I don't think I'd stay with you." I now know those words were uttered by hurting people hurting each other. I remember crying and thinking, *Are Mom and Dad going to be okay? I hope my kids never hear this kind of talk if I ever get married.*

A few days later, I remember walking down a sidewalk behind my parents. My dad extended his big thick hand, and my mother placed her little hand inside of his. That happened when I still thought girls had cooties, but I felt something "fuzzy-wuzzy" going on inside of me that day. I breathed a huge sigh of relief and thought, *Good! They're okay. They love each other. They're back together. They fixed things.*

May I encourage you, doing what needs to be done in the home requires a mom and a dad to effectively work together. I love this particular proverb from my father: children need a mother who will love them and who will listen to them. God gave each person two ears and one mouth; therefore, we ought to catch His hint to listen—especially to our children.

My mother was a listener. I remember coming to her with questions at times. I also knew that both my mother and my dad loved me. My dad felt that it was especially true that teenage boys needed a loud-mouthed dad who would tow the line. Teenage boys need the firmness of the dad, and they need to know their boundaries. When I was growing up, my dad was strict, and he set boundaries.

In Proverbs 4:1-4, Solomon addresses the love of a mom and a dad and shares these truths with his son.

> *"Hear ye children the instruction of a father, and attend to know understanding. [2]For I give you good doctrine, forsake you not my law. [3]For I was my father's son, tender and only beloved in the sight of my mother. [4]He taught me also, and said unto me, Let thine heart retain my words: keep my commandments, and live."*

These verses show the synergy of the home. Because my dad loved me, he gave me commandments to follow. My mom loved me and shared her wisdom with me. In Proverbs 31, Solomon's mother advised him not to drink wine nor strong drink. She warned him not to give his life and strength to immorality. Solomon's mother was very instrumental in the life of this future king. My mother played a very influential part in my life.

3.
WORK DILIGENTLY NOT TO PROVOKE YOUR CHILDREN TO ANGER.

E PHESIANS 6:1 SAYS, *"Children, obey your parents in the Lord: for this is right."* The Devil's greatest desire is to cause dads to be absent altogether from the home. So many men struggle with their temper and being abusive. Distant, withdrawn fathers are disconnected from their children or simply absent altogether. One of Satan's favorite tactics is to get Dad out of the picture so he cannot influence his children for the Lord.

Proverbs 22:6 says that fathers are supposed to train up their children in the way they should go. Colossians 3:21 says, *"Fathers, provoke not your children to anger, lest they be discouraged."* Some children are rebellious because they have been embittered (provoked to anger) by their fathers. A provoked child will lose heart and lose his courage, and every child needs courage.

One way that a father can provoke a child to anger is through teasing. So many fathers like to tease, and I am quick to say that nothing is wrong with teasing in moderation. However, far too many fathers cross the line, and the teasing is no longer funny. In my house, I have a little saying my family follows: "It's not fun if it's not fun for everyone." If it's only fun for one, then it's not fun anymore. Fun should always be a two-way street. Certainly teasing can be a way of provoking a child to anger.

Hypocrisy is another way of provoking children to wrath. Probably the number-one way children are provoked is when their parents struggle with sincerity. Certainly all of us struggle at times with being sincere. Nobody can honestly say, "I've never been a hypocrite." At some time or another, all of us have put on a show and have been insincere. The end result of someone in leadership who says one thing and does something else is anger and frustration. When parents do not keep their word, they create anger and frustration. If we say we're going to do something, we need to keep our word.

I hate to admit that I have been guilty of modeling "do what I say, not what I do," which is so hypocritical. That type of behavior will only generate frustration and rebellion. I hurt my children when I say, "Don't yell!" and I'm yelling.

When parents model the wrong kind of behavior and provoke their children, they need to apologize to them. I have learned to ask my children to forgive me at different times, and I am amazed how quickly my children will do so. They've had a lot of practice!

When we provoke our children to anger with our pharisaical hypocritical conduct, we hurt our children. Many of us provoked our children years ago, but we have never taken the appropriate steps to confess and correct our behavior. When God brings our poor modeling to our mind, we ought to speak back to Him with words of confession and agreement. Then we should take the steps to be right with our children.

4.
LEARN TO LISTEN TO WHAT YOUR CHILDREN HAVE TO SAY.

PSALM 8:2 SAYS, *"Out of the mouth of babes and sucklings hast thou ordained strength because of thine enemies, that thou mightest still the enemy and the avenger."* Most parents need to remember that God gave them two ears and one mouth so they would catch the hint. We need to listen to our children with our eyes, our ears, and our full attention.

Have you ever had one of your children take your head, move it to look directly at them, and then plead, "Dad, listen to me"? That child wants to be heard—really heard—by his or her parent. He doesn't want to hear, "Uh-huh, Uh-huh" as an answer.

My dad listened to us very, very closely and asked many questions. His advice was to listen to what your children have to say because accusations harden the will, but questions soften the conscience. Parents need to learn to ask specific questions. Parents can learn a lot about a situation simply by asking questions and waiting for and letting their children answer.

I remember vividly my father's practicing this particular proverb.

5.

When you know the Lord's will on a matter, call the family together and tell them.

COMPARATIVELY SPEAKING, MY family was poor, and we often had needs. I figured out how poor we were when I was twelve or thirteen years old and was visiting a friend's house. I saw furniture and kitchen appliances my family didn't have, and I saw that four brothers didn't sleep on the same bed in a small room. The children had private rooms.

My family lived a very simple lifestyle because we were poor. When a need would arise, Dad gathered the family together, and he would say, "Let's pray about this." If he knew what God wanted us to do on a particular matter, he would call the family together for a meeting. I can remember times when he would say, "God wants us to increase our giving." He would sometimes say, "I think God wants us to clean the church on Saturday as a family." After attending that Sword of the Lord Conference when I was in the fourth grade, Dad enrolled me in a soul-winning course and made sure I learned all the verses and steps in the plan.

I'm grateful for his example in finding out what God wanted us to do as a family. Many of our family meetings involved our family's serving God in some capacity. *"...As for me and my house, we will serve the LORD"* (Joshua 24:15).

6.
ENDEAVOR TO HAVE FAMILY DEVOTIONS REGULARLY.

PARENTS, TAKE ADVANTAGE of every teachable moment. Sometimes following through on having family devotions can be a challenge. Families function differently today from how they functioned in days gone by, but I do believe, as much as possible, that having a time when families can talk about the things of God is very important to the stability of the home.

Sometimes a dad works nights and cannot be home in the evenings for family devotions. Sometimes because of the busyness of my schedule, I have not been able to consistently lead family devotions every single day. I do believe with God's help that nearly every single day, I and their mother speak to our children about the things of God. For instance, when I was a schoolteacher, I also coached basketball. Oftentimes I had to be at games at nighttime, and I would leave the house when the kids were still sleeping. Nevertheless, in spite of schedule interference, I do believe that I have a responsibility to continue to keep the Word of God in front of my children.

Deuteronomy 6:6, *"And these words, which I command thee this day, shall be in thine heart."* According to this verse, which I have alluded to several times, Christians need to have the Scriptures in their hearts. Verse 7 tells us what God wants us to do after those words are within us: we should teach out of the overflow. Basically, we parents are to teach every child all the time at every available opportunity.

Recently, one of my younger sons and I were going somewhere, and I said, "Son, remind me of what God did to bring you to Christ." Now I have probably asked him that question 25 times since he got saved, but I want to keep the memory fresh in his mind. I want him to remember and to learn to articulate what happened and what God did.

He said, "Dad, I heard the gospel as a kid, and I think I even made a profession of faith, but I just really wondered about that. I nailed it down, and I finally got the assurance of my salvation." I talked to him about how to share that experience with somebody else if he had the opportunity.

Some of our sons are getting ready to leave home. I saw one of them sitting outside in a swing and went out to talk. I sat beside him, and we talked about the Scriptures, about winning people to Christ, and about the position he was accepting at a church. We talked about his ability to work with his hands— hanging drywall and painting. I complimented him about his propensity to coach, to teach, to work hard, and to disciple the people he wins to Christ. As we stood together in the middle of the yard, I put my arm around him, and we prayed that God would help him, strengthen him, keep him clean and pure, and prepare him for whatever He has for him. Talking about the things of God is not always comfortable to discuss, but every child needs someone to teach him the Bible.

Some children do not have a father in their home; they are not fatherless children because they do have a biological father, but they live in a home without their birth father. Some grounded Christians need to lend that single mother a helping hand by spending time with those children to encourage them and to help in some areas. Some of those kids need to hear about the things of God from a man.

Take time to continually talk to your children. Talking about sports is easy, but peace comes when parents talk to their children about God. Talk to them about a Bible verse that blessed you as well as other spiritual matters.

Sometimes families get in a car, turn on the radio, and listen to sports or the news. I wonder, are parents doing that at the expense of being able to spend quality time with their children? Take advantage of these times to learn together.

In all honesty, I'm not a great example of taking full advantage of travel times, but I am glad I had a dad who did talk to me about spiritual matters. Our family always made much of talking about things of the Bible. Doing so is a command of the Lord.

PARENTAL AUTHORITY AND DISCIPLINE

We must face the fact that many today are notoriously careless in their living.... Discipline practically has disappeared. What would a violin solo sound like if the strings on the musician's instrument were all hanging loose, not stretched tight, not "disciplined"?

– A. W. Tozer

1.

WHEN DISCIPLINING YOUR CHILDREN, EXPLAIN WHY YOU ARE DISCIPLINING THEM.

I DON'T THINK I ever had to wonder why I was being spanked! After the spanking, my father and I would have a prayer together. Finally, Dad would let me know he loved me. What I loved about my father's discipline was that when the correction was over, it was over. I am thankful to this day for his loving me enough to discipline me.

My mother would often say, "John, I tried to rear my children so that not only did I love them, but the whole world would love them." Parents will naturally love their own children, but if they want the whole world to love them, they will have to discipline them. Parents will have to stop their children from doing wrong.

My parents never thought throwing a fit was cute. Seeing a child sin was never funny to them. Parents might excuse a child's poor behavior by saying, "Look at my two-year-old stomping and banging his head on the floor. Isn't he cute?" That behavior is certainly not cute when he is 21 and punching holes in the wall, kicking in the side of cars, or knocking out windows. That's what children will escalate to doing unless parents take the responsibility to stop them and speak to them about their poor behavior. Explain why and what the child did wrong. Discipline them. Pray with them and love them through that time. Parents will always love their child no matter what—even if he is in jail some day. Parents will want the whole world to love their children because of the attributes that they instilled in them. Part of achieving that goal means disciplining.

Proverbs 13:24, *"He that spareth his rod hateth his son: but he that loveth him chasteneth him betimes."* What strong terminology! When parents refuse to discipline their child, they might as well say, "Son, I hate you." The truth is, every child wants to be disciplined. They don't like it at the time, but discipline brings the peaceable fruit. Children who are not disciplined rarely have long-term peace. Chastening is not fun for the parents or the child, but afterward it *"...yieldeth the peaceable fruit of righteousness unto them which are exercised thereby"* (Hebrews 12:11).

If you do not discipline your child, you are not showing proper love. *"But he that loveth him, chasteneth him betimes..."* (Proverbs 13:24). The term *betimes*, which is seldom used in today's vernacular, means "early on, early dawn." In other words, early in their lives parents must learn to discipline their children.

Many children can learn three things before they learn to talk correctly.

1) They can learn to obey. They can obey sweetly and immediately with a right spirit.

2) They can learn the difference between right and wrong. They can figure out what *no* means, what *yes* means, what's right, and what's wrong. God exalts righteousness.

3) They can learn respect. They won't even remember the discipline. They will remember what they learned from the discipline. A parent can show he loves his child by teaching him right and wrong. He that chastens the child will have joy of him. A wise son will bring a glad dad and a glad mom as well.

2.
DON'T SPARE THE ROD AND SPOIL THE CHILD.

IF A PARENT says he is going to discipline his child for certain infractions, he should keep his word! Discipline comes straight from the Word of God, and I believe the Bible very pointedly shows that God believes in loving discipline. The fact that the Bible's methodology is so unpopular has caused authorities to struggle with this concept.

Obviously I do not believe in any abuse of children, but in today's climate, spanking is oftentimes considered abuse. My God is not an abusive God! However, some parents do not trust what the Bible says about discipline. Dr. Benjamin Spock, an American pediatrician, author and activist, successfully distorted the biblical concept of discipline and propagated the philosophy of "Just talk to your kids; reason with them instead."

I believe with all of my heart that God has a different idea. He says in Proverbs 22:15, *"Foolishness is bound in the heart of a child; but the rod of correction shall drive it far from him."* Every child is foolish by nature, which means children do dumb things. They stick their fingers in light sockets. They don't listen to their parents. They rebel. They throw fits when they don't get what they want. If those behaviors are not addressed early in their lives, problems will inevitably arise.

My dad believed in loving but firm discipline. Occasionally, he was angry when he spanked us, but such an instance was more the exception than the rule. Most parents will admit to occasionally dealing with a child in anger. I do not believe that correcting in anger is ever the right way to handle a child who needs to be disciplined. Parents should be very careful to deal with their children when they are in full control. James 1:20 says, *"For the wrath of man worketh not the righteousness of God."* A parent will not discipline his child in the right way when he is angry.

Because my dad believed in administering biblical discipline early on, I knew that if I did something wrong, I would be subject to discipline. I loved my dad, so I didn't want to disappoint him. I am very grateful today that when my dad disciplined my siblings and me, he was very stern. Both of my parents disciplined us. I am very thankful that my parents disciplined me by following Bible instruction. The Bible was their manual for discipline.

Proverbs 13:24, *"He that spareth his rod hateth his son: but he that loveth him chasteneth him betimes."* The Bible says that a man or a woman who loves his child will not spare the discipline; he will discipline his child, but parents who hate their children will not discipline them.

Before they can talk, most children can learn to do right, to obey, and to be respectful. Children can learn to obey with the right attitude immediately and sweetly. Before they even learn to talk, children can learn to respect authority. Early on, parents need to give attention to their children when they do something wrong and lovingly help them with discretion, kindness, and prayer, and by explaining what the problem is and why they must deal with this issue. If parents will do their work in the first four years of their child's life, they will have much less work to do after those formative years.

As a rule, most adults remember very few things that happened to them before their fifth birthday. They might remember something very traumatic that happened, but most of them have very little memory of what happened early on in their lives. Moms and dads who love their children will not allow them to continue in unchecked wrong behavior. In doing so, they will hurt their child.

God will discipline adults. The Bible says in Hebrews 12:5, *"...My son, despise not thou the chastening of the Lord, nor faint when thou art rebuked of him."* When God deals with a person, that person should not get angry with Him. God spanks because He loves him. If a person is not disciplined by God, it is because that person is not His child.

Have you ever wondered why unsaved people seem to commit so many wicked acts and never seem to pay any consequences that can be seen? They do not have the same Heavenly Father; their father Satan (John 8:44) does not love them or discipline them. Sin will complicate their lives, but the Devil will not discipline them when they are wrong.

One of the reasons I know I'm saved is that when I do something wrong, God disciplines me. I'm glad He demonstrates His love to me in such a tangible way. Parents who love their children discipline them early on. Proverbs 19:18, *"Chasten thy son while there is hope, and let not thy soul spare for his crying."* While there is an opportunity to help a child and while there is still hope, chasten him.

Personally, I do not enjoy disciplining my children. I hate it, and I have to talk myself into doing what I know God wants me to do. It's easier for me to say, "That's all right. I did that when I was a kid too." But I have a divine responsibility for my children. I want to take advantage of the opportunities to help them while there is hope. Parents, don't let a child's crying cause you to fail to discipline him when he is in need of loving correction.

Wise is the parent who spends time in the book of Proverbs evaluating the principles contained in this book. Proverbs 22:15 says, *"Foolishness is bound in the heart of a child; but the rod of correction shall drive it far from him."* Have you ever found this verse? "Foolishness is bound in the heart of a child, but *a time out* will drive it far from him"? You are probably not familiar with that verse because quite obviously, it's not in the Bible. God ordained discipline to take care of foolishness.

My children have frequently heard me say, "What you did was foolish; God wants you to be wise." Proverbs 10:1 says, *"...A wise son maketh a glad father: but a foolish son is the heaviness of his mother."* God tells parents to discipline when they see foolishness. Discipline is not fun, but God says that discipline drives foolishness out of the one being disciplined.

Proverbs 29:15, *"The rod and reproof give wisdom...."* Rod and *reproof* mean action and verbal instruction. Ephesians 6:4 says, *"And, ye fathers, provoke not your children to wrath: but bring them up in the nurture and admonition of the Lord."* This verse cites both discipline and instruction. Solomon concluded Proverbs 29:15 with a sad statement: *"...but a child left to himself bringeth his mother to shame."*

As a school teacher for a number of years before I was a pastor and as a pastor, I have counseled many families with children. I have seen the end result of disciplined children; they are happier children. Many times my mother would say, "Kids, I don't want your dad and me to be the only ones who love you. We want the whole world to love you." Parents will love their kids no matter what, but every parent should want his children to be a blessing to everybody—not just to them.

People who are loved by many are partially the result of a mom and a dad who dealt with them and disciplined them.

Undisciplined children are frustrating to the people around them. Moms and dads will put up with their misbehaving children. I have watched moms and dads put up with a kid who throws fits. Throwing fits might be cute when a child is three, but tantrums are not cute when they're thirteen. It's never cute for a child of any age to throw a fit or to argue or to disobey. When children are young, they can be trained, but parents must do that training with control, with discipline, and with the Spirit of God's help.

Ecclesiastes 8:11, *"Because sentence against an evil work is not executed speedily, therefore the heart of the sons of men is fully set in them to do evil."* The principle of this verse is to shorten the time from the offense to the discipline. If at all possible, when a child commits an offense, try to deal with the matter in a controlled manner. If the offense makes you angry, take a break, talk to the Lord and don't handle the matter wrongly. An irate person will invariably do the wrong thing when he is angry.

I have disciplined my children in anger, and my children can testify to times when I have lost my temper. Disciplining in anger is to my shame, and it's embarrassing for me to admit that I have done wrong by my children. Most of the time I can get my act together and tell my child that I'm doing this not at him or her, but for him or her. I try to administer correction as soon as possible, and I have made that time factor a prayer request of mine.

One of the number-one rules in my household is that my children must respect their mother. They can give me a hard time and take their chances, but if they give their mother a hard time, I will "cloud up and rain all over them" as soon as I can get to where they are. Because their mother spends more time with them, they will naturally push their mother more than they push me. The Bible says in Proverbs 17:6, "...*the glory of children are their fathers.*" My wife sometimes has to say, "I'm going to have to talk to Dad," and when she does, she sees an immediate change of attitude because of this verse. Children want their dads to be proud of them.

Since boys especially will push their mother, I have stressed the outcome to my sons. "If you want to give me a hard time, knock yourself out, but if you give your mom a hard time, I will do my best to get from where I am to where you are as quickly as possible." In times when Linda has called me in our 25 years of parenting to say, "Honey, we're hitting a wall here, and I need you," I have always been within a few moments of being able to get there and address the situation.

Every child will hit a wall, and every child will have those moments of feeling the need to push his parents all the way. When those times come, the parents need to push back strongly. Parents, don't lose those battles! You and your child need you to win. Every child will push differently. Some children are much more passive, but every once in a while a passive child will exude a strong, rebellious spirit, causing the parent to think, "What in the world?"

Honestly, I have had times of thinking, this child is too hard for me to rear and train and discipline. I just can't do it. But eventually I see the child become sweet, easy to get along with, and so responsive. Early on, I thought, "How could someone be so hardheaded? I don't think I'm going to win this one." Parents, I cannot stress enough that you **must** win! Difficult times will come with child rearing, and every child will come to a place when he is hard and stubborn and when he will want to win. At that point, parents need to say, "God, give me wisdom. Help me know how to win this battle."

Mom and Dad, stay on the same page with each other. Sometimes, being united is not easy to do. I sometimes remind my wife, "You've never been a boy before; you don't know what it's like to be a son." Boys will naturally "push back." For a while, boys can accept their maternal influence, but after a while, they want to break away and experience independence. At that point, a dad is needed so desperately to help them. Much wisdom is needed on the part of both parents.

Thank God that when a father or a mother forsakes us, God picks us up. Single moms and single dads, claim Psalm 27:10, which says, *"When my father and my mother forsake me, then the LORD will take me up."* If both mom and dad are not present in the home, God's grace will help. Dr. Jack Hyles' sweet mother reared him with the help of God. What a beautiful testimony Coystal Hyles was in that area of her life! My heart goes out to single mothers. God can help them and has helped numbers of them rear godly children against the onslaught of Satan, society, and selfish motives.

I wholeheartedly believe that the following statement my dad wrote in his own handwriting is true: "Don't spare the rod and spoil your child. If you say you're going to discipline your child, follow through!"

3.
DON'T LET THEM PLAY ONE AUTHORITY AGAINST ANOTHER.

THE BIBLE TELLS us that when a man and a woman are married, they become one flesh and are unified as a husband and a wife and then as a mother and a father. When I was in school, my dad did not defend me against a teacher. Yes, some teachers were wrong in their actions; my responsibility was not to decide what happened but how I responded to the injustice that took place.

Sometimes God allows injustice to come into the lives of our children to help them and to teach them—not so the parents fight every battle for them. Parents can show their love by helping their children negotiate difficult situations.

4.

DON'T LET YOUR CHILDREN MAKE OR TAKE EXCUSES.

WHEN SOMETHING WAS wrong, my dad did not ask any questions involving why, but he did want to know what we had done. Usually people who are good at making excuses aren't good at anything else. When the *whats* happened, we had to explain something to Dad.

He would say, "John, don't make excuses. Let's just get the job done."

Romans 14:10 says, *"But why dost thou judge thy brother? or why dost thou set at nought thy brother? for we shall all stand before the judgment seat of Christ."*

My dad didn't appreciate an excuse like, "Well, they did it, so I can do it too." My dad was quick to explain that each of us would stand before the judgment seat of Christ; others would not be held responsible for any of our actions. I am not responsible for another's actions; I'm responsible for my side of the fence taking care of me.

5.

DEAL WITH CHILDREN WHEN THEY ACT LIKE THEY ARE SINNING OR DOING SOMETHING THAT IS WRONG.

PROVERBS 22:15 SAYS, *"Foolishness is bound in the heart of a child...."* When a child acts like he is smoking, he is being foolish. When he acts like he is committing some sin, he is being foolish. The Bible says in Proverbs 14:9 that *"Fools make a mock at sin...."* Only a fool thinks sin is funny.

Comedians earn millions making fun of sin, and people foolishly enjoy laughing at sin. Laughing at immorality is foolish. Laughing at the sodomite culture is foolish. Before the world makes a sin acceptable, they want others to laugh at the practice. Long before homosexuality was widely accepted, *Three's Company* was the first sitcom launched to change the minds of Americans from disgust to an acceptance of the practice of homosexuality. Only a fool makes a mock at sin. My dad lived by I Thessalonians 5:22, which says, *"Abstain from all appearance of evil."* My father wholeheartedly emphasized avoiding all appearances of evil.

When my siblings and I were elementary-aged kids, our family visited our grandmother in San Angelo, Texas. While there we attended church. A small convenience store was located adjacent to the church. After church had concluded and while our parents were conversing with family and friends, our cousin invited us to go to the store with him. That store sold candy cigarettes, and we bought some. Together we began to nervously eat them.

I knew that my dad would not be pleased with our having candy cigarettes. I wasn't walking around brazenly acting like I was smoking those candy cigarettes, but I did hide behind the car to act like I was smoking one before I ate it. Guess who saw me? Right there in the church parking lot, my dad saw fit to correct me in such a way that I have never been tempted to look at candy cigarettes since that day.

My dad later explained why he was so unhappy with me. "Son, sin's never funny. It's never cute to act like you're smoking or drinking. Smoking and drinking are never funny. Immorality is never funny. A dirty joke is never funny. I don't care how funny it might seem to be; don't listen to it. If you do happen to hear one, don't repeat it. Sin is never funny."

Parents, I beg you, don't allow your children or teenagers to make fun of sin or to participate in something that is wicked or questionable as fun.

6.
NEVER ALLOW YOUR CHILD TO TALK BACK, THROW A FIT, OR LIE AND GET AWAY WITH IT.

EVERY CHILD WILL at some time talk back. Every child will at some time throw a fit. Unfortunately, this behavior is a part of human nature. Every child will at some time tell a lie.

By the way, never act surprised when your child does something wrong. You also did wrong when you were a child, but by all means, be disappointed. I believe parents can be disappointed without being shocked. Saying, "I can't believe it!" may only elicit a response like, "Well, you did it when you were young." Rather than being surprised, say, "I'm extremely disappointed. I am as disappointed as I can be. I want the best for you." That disappointment should be like a gut punch. Let them know you're disappointed and how you feel because of their decision.

My dad had three categories that were not tolerated: talking back, throwing a fit, and lying. If and when we did something that "fell" into one of these categories (because kids will), Dad quickly dealt with the infraction. He knew he could not let us slide by in any of these areas.

Everyone has seen parents dealing with an 8- to 10-month-old baby (and even older) throwing a fit. People even chuckle, thinking their actions are funny. When a child is 13, that behavior is definitely not cute nor funny. Dealing with that behavior when a child is eight months tells him, "Hey, that behavior will not work and is not acceptable."

If you deal with a child's behavior early on in life, you won't have to spend his adolescent and teen years addressing these three areas. When instances of talking back, throwing fits, or lying arise, you won't have to be as severe if you address them in the early years.

Parents, please do not take this advice as a criticism, but if a mother can be home with her children, her children need her to be home with them when they are little. Some people think, "I'll stay home when they're a little bit older, but we'll do the daycare now because they won't know any different." Children learn more between birth and four years of age than they will learn in any four years of their life, college included. Oftentimes when parents "farm" them out, the child care provider puts them in front of a television or a video. Children growing up know more about video characters than about Mom and Dad!

Once again, this is my opinion, but I know from experience that if moms and dads can give attention to their kids when they're young, dealing with lying, disrespect, and losing their temper will be much easier. All of those sins come naturally. Being disrespectful, for example, is a serious matter to God. Proverbs 30:17, *"The eye that mocketh at his father, and despiseth to obey his mother, the ravens of the valley shall pick it out, and the young eagles shall eat it."* By the way, Proverbs is a good book for parents to absorb during the child-rearing years. This verse shares how serious disrespect is. Both children and adults say a lot with their eyes; they roll their eyes and say, "Whatever." The child or young person who despises obedience and mocks his parents will lose his spiritual vision because of that rebellion and disrespect.

Ecclesiastes 8:11 addresses the power of intervening and confronting sin. Most parents struggle in this area. I struggle with confrontation to an extent because I do not like conflict or confrontation. However, parents need to confront sin. Ecclesiastes 8:11 says, *"Because sentence against an evil work is not executed speedily, therefore the heart of the sons of men is fully set in them to do evil."* This verse teaches that because an offense is not addressed quickly, the heart of the person is hardened to do evil continually.

Failure to confront sin is one of the things that is wrong with today's penal system. A man can kill someone today but not appear in court for a year or more. He is sentenced even later. So much time lapses before he receives his penalty. When judgment is carried out swiftly, people notice and consider whether or not wrongdoing is worth the price. In some countries of the world, stealing is not a problem. No one has to wonder why the citizens do not steal when they see people walking around with a hand cut off. I am certainly not a proponent of that type of judgment, but in those countries, whenever someone is caught doing wrong, the matter is dealt with expeditiously.

Quick understanding also takes place in the life of a child when punishment is swift. When the child does something wrong, his parents should not lose their temper but deal with the matter quickly. I have tried to do that many times as a dad. Deal with the matter in respect and with control. I say something like, "No, sir, we're not doing that. We will fix that right now."

In my home, I have sometimes resorted to some extreme measures to rectify wrongs. I have taught my children to apologize when they have done something wrong to hurt another's feelings. Intervening and confronting is not fun—for me or for my child. At the same time, I know they'll think twice before having that conversation "again."

One time my dad had all of us kids with him at the grocery store. At the checkout, he couldn't find two of us. He finally found the missing two in the produce aisle, where they were eating a vegetable they thought would be good—only to discover they had gotten hot peppers instead of sweet ones. Dad found them because they were screaming and wiping their eyes. Dad thought that whole incident was hilarious. They had already received their just reward!

More than one time, one of my siblings stole something from a store, and my parents found it later. Back to the store we would go, and Dad would make that child pay for the item. My dad would take his child to the manager after personally prepping the manager not to give any sympathy or understanding. Dad wanted that manager to be as strong and as serious as he could possibly be. Dad wanted the child to confess to the manager.

My dad wanted us to understand how terrible sin was by dealing with our sin immediately. He felt that no sin was too little to make a big deal over.

7.
INSIST AND SEE THAT YOUR CHILDREN DO RIGHT.

PARENTS, OUR CHILDREN are just like us; they're sinners. They have a propensity to do wrong, but insist that your children do right because God majors on righteousness. When children are young and before they learn to talk, they can understand the concepts of what is right and how to obey and show respect. To train children when they're little requires spending time with them when they're little. Don't turn them over to someone else to rear or entertain them with a television screen and say, "I'll start investing in them when they start talking." I am sorry to say, that's way too late.

Rather than saying, "That's wrong," help them understand what's right. I don't think that's a terrible way to correct, but try saying, "That's not right. We want to do what's right." Matthew 6:33 says, *"But seek ye first the kingdom of God, and his righteousness; and all these things shall be added unto you."* God majors on righteousness, justice [doing what is right], and judgment.

With every child, doing right has to be learned, and parents can help their child do that. Sometimes teaching your child to do right is not fun. More than one time, I have had to help my children do right.

I have had a parent come to me and say, "Pastor, I hate to

tell you this, but your child did thus and so." Often in dealing with the child, my child and I will get in our car and drive to wherever we need to go. My child and I go together to the door and knock. I ask to speak to the person who has been wronged. I am very forthright and say, "We need to get this situation straightened out."

My children hate it, and I hate it. Having to do right by another person can be embarrassing. I want my children to do right, and I should do whatever it takes to make it right. I say, "My child didn't do right. I'm embarrassed as a father; his mother is embarrassed. I want to apologize to you on behalf of our child. I also want my child to express how badly he feels."

I use the entire drive to teach. We practice making a proper confession and a proper apology. An apology is not a simple "Sorry." "Hey, we okay?" is not an apology. "Can we move on?" is not an acceptable apology.

I John 1:9 says, *"If we confess our sin...."* *Confession* means "to say what I did." Helping your children do what is right is not easy, not convenient, and not popular. It is not taking the path of least resistance. We need a revival of people doing right.

One of the reasons why I tithe is that it's right. God said it's right, so it's right. Someone has said, "Nothing's ever settled till it's settled right." May I adapt that proverb? "Nothing's ever settled right until it's settled right with God." If God says it's right, I need to be disciplined enough to say, "I will do the right thing." Thank God for the opportunity to do what is right.

Micah 6:8, *"He hath shewed thee, O man, what is good; and what doth the LORD require of thee, but to do justly, and to love mercy, and to walk humbly with thy God?"* The phrase *to do justly* means "to do the right thing." We simply do whatever is right to do. Parents in the home need to say, "Our family will do the right thing—not what I feel like doing, not what I want to do, but what is right."

When someone seeking advice shares a certain scenario, ask the person, "What do you think the right thing to do is? What does God want you to do?"

Not too long ago, somebody came to me to complain and gripe about another person. I listened and said, "That's tough. What do you think God wants you to do with that?"

"That's not what I really wanted to hear, Pastor," the person responded.

He finally agreed that what God wanted was what he needed to do. *"There is a way that seemeth right unto a man, but the end thereof are the ways of death"* (Proverbs 16:25). *"As for God, his way is perfect..."* (Psalm 18:30). Each Christian needs to find out what God wants him to do and determine to do right.

Always be committed to doing what's right. Insist on and see to it that your children do what is right in any given situation. They won't like it, they might throw a fit, but work on it till they get the right attitude. Do the right thing.

DEVELOPING RELATIONSHIPS

The world does not
understand theology
or dogma, but it
understands love
and sympathy.

– D. L. Moody

1.
PROVIDE YOUR CHILDREN WITH A GODLY PARENT.

IN II TIMOTHY 1:5, the apostle Paul addresses Timothy personally, saying, "You know the example that your mother Eunice and your grandmother Lois gave for you." Probably the number-one way that parents anger their children and provoke young people to wrath is through hypocrisy. I don't believe anything frustrates kids more than hypocrisy. The Bible says in Ephesians 6:4, *"And, ye fathers, provoke not your children to wrath…."* Statements like "Do what I say—not what I do" are especially provoking. Being one way in front of others and a different way behind closed doors or being one way in church and another way on the way home from church creates great frustration.

I can provide my kids a legacy of godliness even if I may not provide for them the greatest financial abilities. Wise men leave a heritage to their children's children. Basically, my dad left me little financially. For the most part, he died a poor man with little to offer his children financially. However, I can testify that I received far more from my dad than money could ever buy. I had a godly example. I had someone who sacrificed during his entire life to give me a strong Christian heritage for which I am truly grateful.

Some people work hard to save up funds to give their kids, spoiling them with money. Certainly I am not against an inheritance, as I also believe parents have a Biblical responsibility to care for their children financially. I do believe giving your kids an inheritance without an example is robbing them of the greatest blessing they could have.

2.

SHOW LOVE AND AFFECTION TO YOUR SPOUSE IN FRONT OF YOUR CHILDREN.

I BELIEVE THIS proverb of my father is extremely important. The stability and the security of children rests heavily on the stability of their parents' marriage. When parents are crazy about God and are crazy about each other, the kids are much more secure. When Dad and Mom are at odds with each other, the kids can feel that tension and strife.

My parents faced some tough times in their marriage. As a third grader, I remember lying in bed listening to them argue. My dad had been stressed over a situation, and unfortunately, the frustration had carried over into their marriage. I can still remember crying over what I was hearing.

A couple of things happened in my mind that day. In my little elementary-age mind, I said to myself, "I don't ever want my kids to hear this." And I feared for the future, wondering, *Is my family going to be okay?* I was hearing talk like, "If it weren't for the kids, I would be gone!" I honestly wondered if my parents were going to make it. As I look back now, that stressful situation was just a small matter—nothing earth-shattering. But as I lay in bed that night, I wondered, *What's going to happen? Are my parents going to split up?* The thought brought tremendous shock waves of insecurity to my heart and mind.

A few days later I was watching my parents walk down a sidewalk when my dad extended his hand to my mom. She placed her lovely little hand inside of my dad's big hand, and they continued walking hand in hand. When I saw them holding hands, I received the assurance that everything would be all right.

We must learn to show loving affection one to another. In Proverbs 5:15, Solomon instructed his son to make much of his own relationship with his wife. *"Drink waters out of thine own cistern, and running waters out of thine own well."* This verse is saying to find your satisfaction and your joy in the wife that God has given you.

"Let thy fountains be dispersed abroad, and rivers of waters in the streets. Let them be only thine own, and not strangers' with thee. Let thy fountain be blessed: and rejoice with the wife of thy youth" (Proverbs 5:16-18). The Bible says to enjoy the relationship of the wife with whom you fell in love. Keep that relationship close, and don't seek for another.

Ecclesiastes 4:9, 12, *"Two are better than one...and a threefold cord is not quickly broken."* Adding Christ to your marriage makes a threefold cord. Learning to keep Christ in your marriage and in your life together is huge for your children. Be sure to show love and affection to your spouse in front of them.

The marriage relationship is a covenant relationship. No vows are exchanged between parents and children because that relationship is temporary in nature; the marriage covenant is permanent. The marriage relationship is very valuable and should be treasured. Mark 10:7, 8, *"For this cause* [marriage], *shall a man leave his father and mother, and cleave to his wife;* *⁸And they twain shall be one flesh...."* For children to know that Mom and Dad are together is extremely important.

When my wife and I are together, our kids want to be right in the middle—between us! The few times I have had the opportunity to sit with Linda in church, the kids want to sit between us, but we don't let them; they are our "bookends." They don't like being bookends; they want to be the cream in the Oreo—like most kids.

When the children were younger and I planned to take their mother out for a date, I would sing my children a song that they didn't really appreciate! The following are the words I would sing to them:

Children, please give me your kind attention.
I've something to say; here's my intention.
I'm going to go out with your mother tonight,
And it won't matter if you put up a fight.

You may wonder how I could be so thoughtless
To want just your mother and me.
Now she's your dear mother, we know this is true.
She was my sweetheart before there was you.

They did not care for the next verse either:

We're going to walk by the ocean, and we're going
    to hold hands.
We'll write our name in the red sand.
We'll send out "I love you," and send them out in a bottle
And in memory of you children, we're going to eat at
    McDonald's.

You may wonder how I could be so thoughtless
To want just your mother and me.
Now she's your dear mother, we know this is true.
She was my sweetheart before there was you…
And she'll be my sweetheart when there's no more you.

I would sing that song to teach them that mom and dad needed to be together and to love one another.

Notice what the Bible tells the women in the church in Titus 2:4 and 5:

> "*That they may teach the young women to be sober* [to understand their purpose in their home and their church family; to be serious about their purpose] *to love their husbands, to love their children, To be discreet* [not loud and boisterous] *chaste* [pure], *keepers at home* [taking care of the home front], *good* [generous], *obedient to their own husbands, that the word of God be not blasphemed.*"

The Bible tells us that an insubordinate young wife can bring about reasons for the enemy of God to blaspheme.

Learn to show affection. In 1 Peter 3: 1-6, God has a strategy in place for the wife who lives with a husband who does not presently obey or respond to the Word of God. That wife has an opportunity to make a difference. She can be used of God by allowing her testimony to be God's greatest influence on his life.

I Peter 3:7, "*Likewise, ye husbands, dwell with them according to knowledge, giving honour unto the wife, as unto the weaker vessel, and as being heirs together of the grace of life; that your prayers be not hindered.*" This verse is addressing husbands in regard to the wife. *Dwell* means "to spend time with her." Learn her needs. Being a husband is a lifelong opportunity. Only a few moments are needed to become a husband and a wife; a lifetime is required to be good at marriage. Becoming a good spouse means you have to continue learning. The problem is, you have a "moving target" you are learning when you are married. Because both a husband and a wife are changing, a spouse can never leave the school of learning. They must keep asking questions, keep being involved, and keep observing!

Wife, ask the Holy Spirit for wisdom to observe what your husband currently needs. Husbands, what does your wife currently need from you? You may discover that she no longer likes the same candy bar she liked when you were dating. Her taste buds have changed four times since that time! God wants a husband to know his wife and honor her so his prayers won't be hindered.

That moms and dads are affectionate to one another is very important in a marriage. Some people try to excuse themselves by saying, "Well, I just wasn't raised in a family like that." My advice then is to change the cycle of that sin! For children and teenagers to see their parents holding hands and embracing is so good. I am so glad I saw my dad reach out to hold my mom's hand. Their displays of affection were meaningful to me as a child. To me, they were saying without words, "We're okay."

I believe that for children to see affection demonstrated between parents is very natural, very right, and very healthy.

3.
DON'T ALLOW THEM TO RIDICULE THE POOR OR HANDICAPPED.

T HE BIBLE SAYS in Proverbs 22:2, *"The rich and the poor meet together: the Lord is the maker of them all."* God loves the poor and the handicapped. My dad was death on making fun of the poor or handicapped because he loved the underdog—perhaps because he was the son of a drunkard mother and an underdog. If one of us ever thought we were better than another person, Dad was hurt by our attitude. If we ever made fun of a crippled person or someone who was deaf or blind or if we acted like we didn't care for them, Dad would help us understand the sin that caused such actions. Dad would take us to the nursing homes and teach us to greet the people, love them, and help them.

When I was a child, I couldn't stand visiting nursing homes because they all seemed to smell bad to me. When one of my brothers smelled something bad, he would automatically throw up. This happened several times. Our physical issues did not deter my father. Dad would take us to model for us how to love the people. He would push the people in the wheelchairs. He taught us how to help by his example. He modeled the truth that God is not a respecter of persons. He reminded us that only by the grace of God are we what we are and can we do what we do. By the grace of God, you can find your mouth with a spoon today. By the grace of God, you can clothe yourself today.

When I was in the seventh grade, some Christian servants came to our church for two weeks to teach sign language classes each evening. Dad insisted that my sister Janna and I attend them. I was excited about the classes early on, but I didn't want to keep going. When I mentioned dropping out, my dad insisted that I keep going. "John, you started something; you are going to finish it."

Today, my sister Janna is a deaf interpreter. When she and her husband went to Namibia as missionaries, they were eventually exiled from the country. While she and Chris were in South Africa, the people in Namibia who were in the deaf school where Janna had volunteered petitioned the government for their return. They were two of very few missionaries who were able to return to the country—all because she had learned sign language when she was young.

My wife was born in a home with a deaf mother. I have had the joy of communicating with my mother-in-law as her son-in-law and preaching the Gospel numerous times using the tool of sign language.

4.
PLAY WITH YOUR CHILDREN AS MUCH AS YOU CAN.

EPHESIANS 6:4 SAYS, *"And, ye fathers, provoke not your children to wrath: but bring them up in the nurture and admonition of the Lord."* Most dads are busy and have things to do, places to go, and people to see. If they don't work, they're not worth their salt. If they work, they're worth their weight in gold. My dad was a big man—six foot four and usually weighing 270+. Physically he wasn't extremely agile.

One time Dad, my brother, and I were together by a barn on the property where we were living. I was probably in second grade, and my brother was in first grade. We challenged Dad to race to the house. We both got tangled up in his legs, and he fell down. I will always remember how he laughed as we sprawled together on the ground in that West Texas dirt. We were laughing even though we had skinned up our hands and knees, but I felt so bad for my dad. Nevertheless, I have never forgotten the fact that he would try to run a race with my brother and me.

He loved to play ball with us—especially softball. He would generally pitch the softball because he had a lame shoulder. He wanted my brothers and me to participate in sports, and he would faithfully attend our basketball games and things of that nature. Anytime we could get together and have a good time, Dad was in the thick of things. I thank the Lord for my dad's playing and enjoying free time with my siblings and me.

5.

BE CAREFUL TO KEEP PROMISES MADE TO CHILDREN UNLESS PROVIDENTIALLY HINDERED.

SOMETIMES YOU SIMPLY cannot keep a promise. When you say, "We're going to do this" and something else comes up, an explanation needs to be made. Do your very best to keep commitments and promises. In fact, be very careful about using the words "I promise." The Bible says in Matthew 5:37, *"But let your communication be, Yea, yea; Nay, nay...."* In other words, say yes and no. When you say, "I swear on a stack of Bibles," what you are saying is, "You can't trust me all of the time, but you can this one time."

When someone says, "I promise, I promise, I promise..." what he is saying is "I'm promising you this time; the other times I wasn't telling you the truth. You can believe me this time." If you tell your child you're going to do something, make sure you try to make that happen.

My dad wasn't a perfect dad, but if he told the family he was going to do something, I could count on it. Dad was going to do it. He would find a way to keep that commitment. At times the plan went awry, and things did not go the way he would have liked for them to happen. But when those times happened, he would invariably call us together and say, "Guys, I'm sorry. I told you I was going to do that, but now we can't. We'll do it later because this time it will not work, or we can try something else comparable." He would often go into further explanation.

We understood when he took time to explain. He didn't simply say, "Forget what I said; we're not doing that." That kind of flippant answer only creates anger and frustration. Try to keep promises or commitments you've made unless you are providentially hindered by an act of God.

Proverbs 13:12, *"Hope deferred maketh the heart sick: but when the desire cometh, it is a tree of life."* The word *hope* is used in this verse to mean when you have your heart set on something or you expect something will happen because of what you were told.. In Bible times, hope was more like a guarantee based upon the Word of God or based upon someone's word. That definition of hope is why God tells us *"And now abideth faith, hope, charity, these three; but the greatest of these is charity"* (I Corinthians 13:13).

In this day and age, Christians operate by hope. Titus 1:2 says, *"In hope of eternal life, which God, that cannot lie, promised before the world began."* *Living in hope* means "I'm living and trusting in what God said." I am trusting the guarantee that I have the eternal life that God gave me in the Scriptures. I will go to heaven based upon that hope. God cannot lie (Numbers 23:19); He will not change His mind (Malachi 3:6), so every believer has the hope of eternal life.

The hope mentioned in Proverbs 13:12 means that a child or a person hopes he has someone's word to do something, but when that hope is sidelined, put off, or changed, the result is a sick heart. When a child's heart (emotions) is ill, healing love and humility are needed.

BUILDING FRIENDSHIPS

Happy is the man who has a
friend. Happier is the man
who is a friend. Happiest is
the man who has a friend
and is a friend.

– Jack Hyles

1.
TEACH YOUR CHILDREN PRINCIPLES OF FRIENDSHIP.

Some Fundamentals of Friendship

I WAS PREPARING to preach in Lebanon, Missouri, when a man walked up to me, shook my hand, and introduced himself by saying, "I was your dad's roommate in college; my name is...."

Before he could give his name, I interrupted him and said, "Your name is Scott Miller, and my dad talked about you often." I think he might have been somewhat surprised that I already knew who he was.

"Your father was such a good friend to me, and I am so grateful," he said.

I knew this man's name because my dad had talked about him through the years. My dad lived by the next principle I want to share, and he made sure that his children learned it. No one is all that he should be in this area, but my dad really worked on teaching his children this principle. "Now, John," he would say to me, "I want you to be a friend to everybody. Don't just hang out with the cool kids. You go sit with the new kid in Sunday school; don't ignore him and sit with your group. You make that boy feel welcome. Son, I want you to decide you're going to be a welcoming committee of one."

Because of my dad's teaching, I have since made the statement, "Be a welcoming committee of one" countless times. I often encourage people to find a way to be a help and a blessing to someone, to go out of their way to be friendly, and to invite someone to their house—to decide to be a welcoming committee of one.

The home in which I was reared was a revolving door. People would eat with us, and they would stay with us. My dad was a friend to his friends. Being a first-generation Christian, Dad taught me what he was also learning. One lesson was to be a good friend. Some of the principles he taught us on being a good friend are found in Proverbs 27.

1) **Don't take your friendships for granted.** Verse 1 says, *"Boast not thyself of to morrow; for thou knowest not what a day may bring forth."* When I was preparing this chapter, our church family had just said goodbye to a 34-year-old lady. Most people will live past the age of 34. Since no one has a guarantee on life, perhaps he should ask himself the following questions:

- "What am I really doing with my life?"
- "How am I treating my loved ones?"
- "Am I able to write a note to a loved one?" If so, my friend, write it today!
- "Am I able to call my loved ones?"
- "Am I able to give?"
- "Am I able to serve?"
- "Am I able to encourage others, especially a friend?"

Do it today! If so, don't say, "Well, I'll do it next week." You don't know that you will have that opportunity next week. Don't take your friendships for granted.

2) **Being a good friend means not bragging on yourself.** *"Let another man praise thee, and not thine own mouth; a stranger, and not thine own lips"* (Proverbs 27:2). No one enjoys

fellowshipping with people who always talk about themselves. If you are skilled in a certain area, let someone else say that about you rather than your feeling the need to say, "I can do this." "I can dribble, and I can dunk the ball." "I can spike this." "I make straight A's." Let someone else praise your merits. People who constantly talk about themselves usually end up somewhere alone sitting in a corner with no friends and wondering, "Why don't I have any friends?" The answer is simple: you spent your whole life thinking and talking about yourself.

3) **To be a good friend, learn to master your temper.** *"A stone is heavy, and the sand weighty; but a fool's wrath is heavier than them both"* (Proverbs 27:3). The Bible says of angry people: *"Make no friendship with an angry man..."* (Proverbs 22:24). Angry men do not make good husbands or loving fathers. Angry ladies do not make sweet wives and godly mothers. Folks who struggle with anger usually have a limited number of friendships. Too many times I have counseled with people who say, "I don't have any friends." At some point in our conversation, they'll throw a fit right in front of me, and I will say, "That's why you don't have any friends. You're angry!" Sometimes the person will even retort, "I don't have any friends, and you'd be mad too if you didn't have any friends." If you want to have friends, then deal with your anger issues! You will become more of a magnet than a repellent.

4) **Guard against envy.** Proverbs 27:4 states, *"Wrath is cruel, and anger is outrageous; but who is able to stand before envy?"* Losing your temper is cruel; everyone is on edge around an angry person. The act of jealousy takes place when something happens to somebody else and another says, "I wish that had happened to me." Envy goes a step beyond jealousy. Being envious is more like, "If something good can't happen to me, I

don't want it happening to you." An envious person wants the good to be taken away from another.

Years ago my brothers and I were out fishing, and one of my younger brothers caught a big fish. I was 12 or 13 years old at the time. Because he always seemed so lucky, I "accidentally" let that big fish go. If I couldn't catch a fish, I didn't want him to walk home and show Mom and Dad that he had. To this day, I feel terrible and am embarrassed that I purposely hurt my brother like I did. That personal illustration aptly describes envy—the green-eyed monster. Displaying envy will keep you from having friendships.

Oftentimes the enemy of contentment is comparison. We tend to forget that God has been very good to all of us. Unfortunately, we struggle with contentment when we start looking around and thinking, "But I don't have what that person has." When a person starts comparing himself with somebody else, he will lose his contentment. Jealousy and envy will start spiking in his life and complicating his friendships.

5) **Be truthful and helpful to your friend.** *"Faithful are the wounds of a friend; but the kisses of an enemy are deceitful. The full soul loatheth an honeycomb; but to the hungry soul every bitter thing is sweet. As a bird that wandereth from her nest, so is a man that wandereth from his place. Ointment and perfume rejoice the heart: so doth the sweetness of a man's friend by hearty counsel."* (Proverbs 27:6-9) These verses refer to interacting with your friends. *"Faithful are the wounds of a friend..."* illustrates the truth that a real friend stabs his friend in the front; he doesn't stab him in the back. A real friend will occasionally hurt his friend with something he sees in his life that needs to be adjusted or changed.

When a person doesn't have a relationship with someone

else, it's very difficult to confront that person with issues. When it becomes necessary to correct someone, that person will not take the correction well because he doesn't think he is loved by the one doing the correcting. A real friend will occasionally wound his friend with some corrective words. The person who has a friend always in agreement with him probably does not have a real friend. When he says, "I got so angry I told the person off," the wrong kind of "friend" will say, "Oh, that's what I would do too. Way to go!" A real friend would say, "Have you listened to yourself? Is that right? Do you think God was honored with what you said?" Good friends are very careful about giving correction.

Indeed, at times a true friend needs to keep his nose out of his friend's business. *"...As a bird that wandereth from her next, so is a man that wandereth from his place"* (verse 8). Each person should stay on his side of the fence because unsought advice is seldom heeded and usually resented. I have heard people say, "I think I was off my rug, but I had to tell them." Maybe that person should have stayed on his rug and not risked hurting his friend.

6) **Step in when others step out.** *"Thine own friend, and thy father's friend, forsake not; neither go into thy brother's house in the day of thy calamity: for better is a neighbour that is near than a brother far off"* (Proverbs 27:10). We need to be the kind of friends who are there to help in times of need. Whenever people need help, don't forget them. Try to assist hurting people.

7) **Gravitate to the underdog and the outcast.** My dad was a master at following this principle. Perhaps my father gravitated to those who were having the hardest time because of the way he was reared. If he knew someone would not be chosen on a team, he would choose that person, and he might

even pick that person first. He didn't want the person to deal with the feelings of what it was like to be chosen last. He would find somebody at church who was struggling, and he would sit with the person.

Dad would always and invariably send me to the underdog. Sometimes I would go on a field trip when Dad had volunteered to drive the bus. When he spotted a boy alone, he would say, "John, go over and sit with him." When I would sometimes protest, he would say, "No, go sit with him. Make him feel like he's special. No excuses."

Gravitating to the underdog or outcast doesn't come naturally, and I'll be honest, I didn't want to do what my dad said! My children don't want to do that, and in all likelihood, you don't want to do that either. We want to go places and be with people we like and who like us. We don't want to go toward people when we have to take a risk. We oftentimes tend to gravitate toward people of similar background, but I do believe that following biblical friendship principles means learning to help people who are different than we are.

Years ago Dr. Jack Hyles said that not one young person would ever go wrong if he knew that one person sincerely cared about him. The Devil has been so ruthlessly successful in causing many young people to taste the bitterness of rejection. Some of these rejected ones are beautiful, cultured, refined, gifted people who suffered from rejection during childhood. Causes are multiple, and almost everybody who has challenging situations has reasons why. Many of us do not understand those who have faced rejection. Most of us have some difficult days, but very few bad, bad days. We must learn to gravitate to hurting people.

Parents, this principle can be mentored and taught, but

gravitating to the needy also must be modeled. Much is taught through mentoring, but more is taught through modeling. The 1920s gave Americans a saying that remains true today: "Monkey see, monkey do." If you do it, your kids will do it. "Do what I say—not what I do" will not work. That attitude only breeds frustration and rebellion. Parents must mentor their children but major on modeling what they teach.

8) **Be sensitive and do not take advantage of your friendships.** *"He that blesseth his friend with a loud voice, rising early in the morning, it shall be counted a curse to him"* (Proverbs 27:14). Always be sensitive to how others are feeling. Be careful and considerate of your friends. Being insensitive is rude and inconsiderate.

9) **Strengthen and encourage your friends.** *"Iron sharpeneth iron; so a man sharpeneth the countenance of his friend"* (Proverbs 27:17). On purpose, decide to strengthen and encourage your friends. We are happy when some people walk into the room; we are happy when others walk out! Some of us hurt people because we are hurting ourselves. Hurting people tend to hurt people. That feeling has much to do with whether or not that person cares about others and sharpens others. Some folks are like ticks or leeches; they constantly drain other people. Their texts are draining, their calls are draining, so they're always needy. Mature Christians learn to handle those personalities.

God says that iron sharpens iron; so a man sharpens the countenance of his friend. Seeking to improve one's self and others by provoking each other to love and to good works will sharpen a person—making him better for the Master's use. When people come to you, they should leave feeling, "Being around this person makes me happy. I have been encouraged and strengthened."

2.
TRAIN YOUR CHILDREN TO BE FRIENDLY TO EVERYONE.

PROVERBS 18:24 SAYS, *"A man that hath friends must shew himself friendly: and there is a friend that sticketh closer than a brother."* Learning to be friendly is not natural. Sometimes, but not always, people who are shy are demonstrating prideful behavior in failing to care for another. Saying, "Well, I just don't talk to people" may be prideful because the Bible says that a person who has friends must show himself friendly.

Do you honestly think Jesus walked through a crowd with a frown? Do you really think mothers would bring their babies and little children to Someone who would say, "Leave Me alone! What are you doing bringing your children to Me?" No, of course not! His countenance and aura were very inviting. *"But the wisdom that is from above is first pure, then peaceable, gentle, and easy to be intreated, full of mercy and good fruits, without partiality, and without hypocrisy"* (James 3:17). Jesus was very approachable. Likewise, parents need to teach their children to be approachable. Children need to learn to be friendly.

My parents would take me to nursing homes, but I did not like going to nursing homes. Even now, I do not find them to be a comfortable environment, but I regularly visit in nursing homes in order to be a blessing to people because God loves people through us. When I was a child, I was afraid of the people because I didn't know how to deal with them. My dad wanted his children to have a heart for people, so he developed that attitude by taking us to nursing homes and by having us in the bus ministry. Often, when we would go bus calling, he would say, "Why don't you go talk to that young boy or girl? I want to talk to the mom and dad. You go talk to him or her."

My first response was, "I don't want to do that. I don't even know this kid."

No matter how much my siblings and I would hold back, he would continually encourage, "Go talk to them." Too many young people just stand around playing on their phone while everybody else is doing something. What an indifferent response! We must teach our children to be friendly and to use their God-given gifts for eternal purposes.

The Bible is teaching in I Peter 4:8-10 that every person has a gift—a strength.

> *"And above all things have fervent charity* [a hot love and care] *among yourselves: for charity shall cover the multitude of sins. Use hospitality* [being friendly using what I have to help somebody else, generosity, caring for other people] *one to another without grudging* [not being upset about it; getting to do it, not "I have to do it."]. *As every man hath received the gift, even so minister the same one to another, as good stewards of the manifold grace of God."*

According to this passage, every child is gifted. He is to operate in his strength even as he strives for all of the gifts. Thrive in one; strive for all.

The seven gifts in Romans 12 are 1) prophecy, 2) ministry, 3) teaching, 4) exhortation (or encouraging people), 5) mercy, 6) giving, 7) ruling.* Every person has a strong gift in at least one of those seven areas. Parents should teach their children to thrive in one but strive for all. I admire parents who strive to develop their child's talent. When the child is near a piano and starts banging on the keys, many say, "Stop! That noise is driving me crazy." Some parents see that dissonant noise as an aptitude and continue to help their child grow and learn in that area.

When a child has an obvious strength, parents ought to say, "What can we do to strengthen our child's gifts for the Lord Jesus Christ? How can we help him with that? In the same way, we need to help our children be friendly as they use their strengths. We often don't want to go out of our comfort zone to greet and befriend. We are not used to leaving our comfort zone to be gracious, kind, and giving to other people.

God put children in our homes so we could help them learn to be need fillers. Help your children develop their God-given gifts. You make a living by what you get, but you make a life by what you give. Teach them that philosophy. Developing your God-given gifts is a way to give to others. Those who give will be rewarded for eternity with Jesus. Matthew 6:20 says, *"But lay up for yourselves treasures in heaven...."* That verse can apply not only to how a person uses his money but also to how he uses his talents and his gifts.

NOTE:

Book 7 in Level 3 of the Foundations of My Faith discipleship series shares an explanation of these spiritual gifts. These booklets are available through gracetogrowpublications.com.

3.
CHOOSE YOUR CHILDREN'S FRIENDS.

M Y FATHER WAS probably one of the strictest people I know in this area. He was very careful about the friends my siblings and I chose. Quite possibly, following this proverb may have been the second-most important guideline my dad set for my siblings and me. He carefully guarded our influences and did not allow us to fellowship with others who entertained bad habits. His number-one priority was that his children attend and be involved in the local church. I can list so many blessings that resulted from that requirement alone. When you have a youth pastor and a pastor and a Sunday school teacher, going to church catapults your spiritual life. There you have the preaching of God's Word, the singing of God's songs, and the opportunity and the provocation to give to the Lord.

Second to that priority, my dad watched carefully the friendships that I kept. My father wrote these proverbs for child rearing, but this priority is also true for everybody. *"For we cannot but speak the things which we have seen and heard"* (Acts 4:20). Paul told the Galatian believers, *"Ye did run well..."* and the next word is *who—"who did hinder you...?"* (Galatians 5:7). When you see someone going in the wrong direction, you'll almost always find a who. Very few people smoke a cigarette for the first time by themselves. Very few people take a drink of alcohol for the very first time by themselves. Very few people look at and do drugs for the very first time by themselves. Nearly always somebody in their way has influenced them. A parent's job is to help his children watch out for the "whos" that could be negative influences.

Another verse to consider is Proverbs 13:1, which says, *"A wise son heareth his father's instruction: but a scorner heareth not rebuke."* Dad, do your children listen to you? Do they listen to their mom? Do your children hear your words of wisdom? God gave them two ears and one mouth; help them catch the hint! The Bible says a wise son listens to his father's instruction.

"He that walketh with wise men shall be wise: but a companion of fools shall be destroyed" (Proverbs 13:20). In this verse, God shows His children wisdom in three ways: 1) The Word of God, 2) Wise people, and 3) The reproofs, challenges, or mistakes of life. Whenever you or I make mistakes, we can learn wisdom. We say, "I'm not doing that again." We learn wisdom whenever we open the Word of God and let someone teach us the Bible, which is a source of wisdom. We learn wisdom by the influence of other wise people.

Seek the companionship of people known for their godly wisdom. Do your children's friends make them better? Several times in the epistles, the Bible says, *"Be not deceived...."* Galatians 6:7 says, *"Be not deceived; God is not mocked: for whatsoever a man soweth, that shall he also reap."* I Corinthians 15:33 says, *"Be not deceived: evil communications corrupt good manners."* Be not deceived (don't kid yourself)! If you hang around somebody who is not a godly influence and is negative and worldly, that association will affect the way you live, as well as your attitude.

My father would always catch my wrong attitudes, and I could not understand how he knew. When I was a teenager, he would look across the landscape of our youth group and pay attention to those I was spending time with. He could peg kids. Perhaps he had the gift of prophecy. He could tell. He would say, "John, do you see so and so?"

"Yeah. He's a good guy, Dad," I would defend my friend.

He would reply, "No, he's not. He's not a boy to admire, so stay away from him. You be nice to him, and you be gracious to him, but I don't want you spending more than thirty seconds with him. Don't go to his house and don't eat lunch with him."

I would argue, "Come on, Dad. Really, he's not that bad."

One day I was driving home after work around 12:30 at night, and I saw my friend's car in the park. I wondered what was going on at the park, so I drove over to where he was standing with some other guys, and they were drinking alcohol. When my "friend" saw me, he called, "Hey, John! You want one?"

"Are you kidding me?" I asked. "No! I'm very disappointed." I felt kicked in the gut to see that behavior after I had believed in him and defended him. As I headed home in my 1974 pickup truck, I thought, *Man, my dad's smart. He knew that guy was a negative influence. He told me, "You can't lay with dogs and not get fleas."*

Young people cannot hang around the wrong kind of influence and handle it. That's exactly what the Bible says when using the words: *"Be not deceived...."* Your friends will affect your conduct.

Romans 16:17, *"Now I beseech you, brethren, mark [or identify] them which cause divisions and offences contrary to the doctrine which ye have learned; and avoid them."* Identify people who live contrary to the way we should live, who cause divisions, and who are rebellious. Get away from them! If you walk with wise men, you'll be wise. If you're a companion with fools, you'll be destroyed.

Years ago I was mentoring a young man whose name was Edgar. He was a good boy whose parents were faithful to the church and the work of the Lord. Edgar had a lovely younger sister and an older sibling as well. One day I saw Edgar hanging around the wrong kind of boys, so I said to him, "Edgar, you're a good boy, but you're hanging around with some bad influences. Be careful!"

He replied, "Pastor, you don't know them. My friends are good guys. You just don't understand them."

A few weeks later I found out that Edgar had been incarcerated. I went to visit his mom and dad and pray with them. Edgar was eighteen years old at the time. He had been riding with friends when one of them pulled out a gun and shot at somebody outside of the vehicle. The police chased them; the other two boys ran away, but Edgar got caught and was arrested. Still cocky, he thought, "I'm okay. I didn't do anything; I didn't touch the gun. They don't have anything on me. I didn't even know the gun was there." Then he received a message from those good guys—those guys I just didn't understand. They notified him in no uncertain terms, "You rat us out, and we're killing your little sister." He believed them, pleaded guilty, and stayed in jail for three and a half years for something he didn't do—all because of hanging around bad friends.

I believe this same illustration could be told multitudes of times—with different places and different names. Parents must not allow their kids to hang around the wrong kids. Parents, it's your job to watch for the bad influences in your children's lives.

II Samuel 13:1, 2 tells the unfortunate story of a king's son, Amnon, who became infatuated with his half-sister, Tamar. "*It came to pass after this, that Absalom the son of David had a fair* [beautiful] *sister, whose name was Tamar; and Amnon the son* of David loved her. *And Amnon was so vexed* [miserable], *that he fell sick for his sister Tamar; for she was a virgin: and Amnon thought it hard for him to do anything to her.*" He was saying, "There's just no way I could ever do anything to hurt her." But the next few words of verse 3 tell a different story: *"But Amnon had a friend...."* What really ruined that young man's life, eventually caused his own death and brought about the defiling of his sister was the counsel of a friend.

We Christians need to learn with all gravity how to choose our friends. We need to be careful about whom we hang around with. Our associations, the people with whom we spend time, what we read, and the people we follow require careful consideration. If they are not good for us, we need to make changes. Don't try to kid yourself and think, *I can handle it.*

Perhaps the second greatest way my father helped me grow my faith outside of church involvement was watching my choice of friends by either encouraging or discouraging the friendship. I want to encourage every parent to do likewise. Let me warn you in advance: your children won't understand. I didn't understand. I even rebelled against some of his hard opinions. When my dad said, "No, you can't stay overnight there" or "You can't be with that young person," I asked, "Why?" To this day, I'm glad my dad was strong and did not give in when I vigorously questioned and doubted his wisdom.

I was visiting my mother recently, and in a moment of reminiscing, she said, "John, I'm so glad that your father was hard on you. Sometimes he was harder on you than I wanted him to be, but now looking back, I'm so grateful that he walked guard on your friends."

4.

Don't let your children stay overnight with a family that is worldly.

M Y DAD WAS in charge, and he was very serious about this proverb. At times he would allow me to go with a friend or spend some time with someone who didn't have the same biblical standards that my dad had. I could go to the person's house for a few hours but never for overnight. Some people never let their child stay overnight with anyone, and I admire that stand though I do think sometimes it may not always be practical.

If someone was worldly or didn't have the same standards of holiness that my dad wanted for me, he would find a way for the invitation not to be convenient. When he would express his regrets, sometimes people became upset and would say, "What's wrong? Are we not good enough for you?"

He might answer, "Our kids are just not good together." My father would rather hurt someone else's feelings than take the risk of hurting his children.

I was spending an afternoon with a family when the dad came up with a different plan than expected. He said, "Hey, guys, I'd like to take you to see *Star Wars.*"

Truthfully, I really wanted to see Star Wars, but I said, "You know what? You'd better call my dad and ask him."

I heard him talking to my dad. "Hey, Mr. Wilkerson, I'm

with the kids, and I was wondering if I could take them to the drive-in to watch *Star Wars.*"

My dad answered like I thought he would. He told the dad that he didn't have a problem with their going to see Star Wars, but he would come by to pick up John. I knew Dad would rather that I not go. I had never been to a movie theater, and I knew Dad did not want me to be exposed to that atmosphere, so he came to pick me up.

I heard my friend's dad protest, "Oh, no, no! We don't have to go the movies. I just thought it might be something we could do. I might need to talk to you more about that later. You don't go to movies?"

I feel certain that he and my dad did talk at some point in time. By the way, I think that my dad's standard is still a good standard. Of course, back then Netflix, videos, and Redbox were not available. I do realize that oftentimes these venues can be very filthy as well. At the movie theater, a spectator cannot turn off something that should not be seen. He cannot stand up in the middle of a theater and say, "Stop! Stop the film. They are using profanity." Cursing is only the beginning of the reasons to turn off a program—instances of immorality take place on the silver screen as well.

The Bible is very definite concerning not only what we do, but also that you *"Let not then your good be evil spoken of"* (Romans 14:16). I have used this verse before, but it bears repeating: *"Abstain from all appearance of evil"* (I Thessalonians 5:22). When a child of God chooses to attend a movie at a theater, he is representing the Lord Jesus Christ.

Certainly I also think Christians must be careful what they see in their own homes nowadays. Some people would even say, "Going to the theater doesn't matter. After all, we will eventually see the same thing in our home in the near future. We might as well go see it in the theater."

To the person who would justify going to the theater, why doesn't he ask God what He wants him to do? I would suggest that you decide not to go to movie theaters. My dad was serious about that matter because of II Corinthians 6, which addresses spiritual separation. II Corinthians 6:14 says, *"Be ye not unequally yoked together with unbelievers: for what fellowship hath righteousness with unrighteousness? and what communion hath light with darkness?* And verse 17 continues, *"Wherefore come out from among them, and be ye separate, saith the Lord, and touch not the unclean thing; and I will receive you."* Does this verse conclude, "...and I will love you"? No! God always loves all of His children. He is not always pleased with all of His kids, but He loves all of them.

I have discovered that when my children are not doing right, they don't want to be where I am. Sometimes it's very hard for me to be with them because they're in rebellion. God said to separate from people who are counterproductive to your Christian life. Verse 18 says, *"And will be a Father unto you, and ye shall be my sons and daughters, saith the Lord Almighty."*

I John 2:15, *"Love not the world, neither the things that are in the world...."* The word *world* used in this verse is not referring to people; rather, the verse is focusing on the world system. Every Christian has common enemies:

1) The world (the society in which he lives)
2) The flesh (self)
3) The Devil (Satan).

All three are counterproductive. Even if the Devil fell off the planet today, we would still have a problem with sin tomorrow because one of our biggest problems is us. Because *"...the flesh lus-teth against the Spirit...,"* walking with God is always a challenge.

We all have issues with our flesh. The world's system is also one of our enemies, and the Bible commands us not to love the world. Christians should create a distance between how this world lives and how they live.

I recently talked to a man who has two doctor's degrees, as well as three other earned degrees. This man could buy me several times over, but he is languishing in a nursing home. As time passes by, he needs to prepare for death and where he will spend eternity. He can no longer stand up and talk in a courtroom and mount a defense. He cannot open a newspaper and see his name in print because he successfully prosecuted or defended another case. That life is now in his rearview mirror. He's trying to figure out his purpose during these last days. All he has are his past laurels. The truth of the matter is, at the age of 89, a person is unable to rest on his laurels. This man's purpose in life was slipping away, and he is living in darkness. What does he need? He needs to respond to the Spirit of God upon his dark heart. *"And God said, Let there be light."* God is the only One Who can bring light.

Paul said it like this in Colossians 3:2, *"Set your affection on things above, not on things on the earth."* Matthew 6:20 instructs the Christian to *"...lay up for yourselves treasures in heaven...."* The Bible constantly challenges every believer to look to the eternal. However, we tend to be very caught up with what's going on in the attractiveness of this world. When most of us walk into our home this evening, the very first thing we do is turn on our lights and reach for the remote control to let the world tell us what's going on. We do not realize that we are allowing the world to dictate our fears, our attitudes, and our actions.

Some of us say, "Well, I need to have noise," but the world's noise is the wrong kind. Instead, we should be creating distance between us and the world. You cannot love God and love the world. You cannot love flowers and not hate weeds; you cannot love God and not hate that which is counterproductive to your relationship with Him.

Romans 16:17, *"Now I beseech you, brethren, mark them which cause divisions and offences contrary to the doctrine which ye have learned; and avoid them."* Mark them means "to identify those within one's sphere of life who cause divisions or whose conduct is contrary to the teaching of the doctrines of God's Word." The book of Proverbs tells the Christian to go from the presence of a fool. Let him sit by himself and don't hang around him. *"He that walketh with wise men shall be wise: but a companion of fools shall be destroyed"* (Proverbs 13:20). I do realize that feelings will be hurt, but separation is a biblical principle and one of the most beautiful doctrines in the Bible.

The way a person lives as a Christian should be distinctively different from the world. How he talks, how he acts, and what he does should be different. People ought to be able to see by a person's countenance that something is different in his life.

To be sure that our family remained distinctively different from the world, my dad set some rules. One of them was, "Don't let your kids go overnight with a friend or spend time with a family that does not share your convictions or has worldly attitudes, actions, or associations." God believed in separation, so we should make the needed separation when biblical principles demand it.

5.

TEACH YOUR CHILDREN NOT TO BE IN THE WRONG PLACE WITH THE WRONG CROWD AT THE WRONG TIME.

P ROVERBS 13:20 SAYS, *"He that walketh with wise men shall be wise: but a companion of fools shall be destroyed."* My father was absolutely all over this rule. As a seventeen-year-old, I didn't like to hear his correction about my friends. I thought I was cool and had all the answers to life and living. My dad stressed that the person who walks with wise men will be wise. He would say, "Fool around with foolish people, John, and you will face destruction."

In Proverbs 7:6-9, Solomon is telling his son about something he viewed.

> *"For at the window of my house I looked through my casement, ⁷and beheld among the simple ones, I discerned among the youths, a young man void of understanding. ⁸Passing through the street near her corner; and he went the way to her house, ⁹In the twilight, in the evening, in the black and dark night."*

Very few good things happen late at night. When do most assaults and murders normally happen in large metropolitan areas? After dark, in the middle of the night. I often wonder why the victims were out so late at night. I do realize that some entirely innocent people work late, and they sometimes are victims of violence through no fault of their own. This young person Solomon mentioned was in the wrong place at the wrong time, going with the wrong people. He was "captured" by an immoral, perverse woman, and the rest is history. Watch out where you are and whom you are with!

I Corinthians 15:33, *"Be not deceived: evil communications corrupt good manners."* Don't kid yourself. The company you keep will affect the way you act. Every child and even adults need to heed that warning. People who fall for bad doctrine have usually been reading a blog or a book, following a person, or listening to a questionable friend. Make sure you keep good company. Don't be in the wrong place at the wrong time with the wrong crowd.

AVOIDING WORLDLINESS

A true revival means nothing
less than a revolution,
casting out the spirit of
worldliness and selfishness,
and making God and
His love triumph
in the heart
and life.

– Andrew Murray

1.

HELP YOUR CHILDREN HAVE THE RIGHT KIND OF HEROES— GODLY MEN AND WOMEN.

J EREMIAH 5:5 SAYS, *"I will get me unto the great men...."* Proverbs 13:20 says, *"He that walketh with wise men shall be wise: but a companion of fools shall be destroyed."* When other preachers or other men of God were in the area, my father would take the family to their meetings. When I was in the fifth grade living in Freeport, Illinois, I remember well the time Bro. Lester Roloff preached in our church. A deacon had become upset when Bro. Roloff stood on the front pew of the church while he was preaching! At the end of the service, Bro. Roloff announced, "I need to go from here to Shannon, Illinois, to preach this afternoon. Can anybody give me a ride?"

My dad's hand went up, and I immediately thought, "Oh, no. We're going to have the preacher ride with us."

Dad turned to us and said, "John, Matt, go out and clean the car." So the two of us hurriedly cleaned the car as best we could. My dad drove, Bro. Roloff rode in the front passenger seat, and my mother and the rest of us sat in the back. Bro. Roloff sang much of the way to Shannon, Illinois! My dad was a big guy, and Bro. Roloff was a small fellow. Bro. Roloff would comment on some matter, hit Dad's arm, and say, "Hey, how about that?" We loved every minute of that trip and thought it was great that we took Bro. Roloff where he needed to go.

Years later I visited with Bro. Roloff at his home in Corpus Christi. He served me some watermelon under his carport. I reminded him of that time when I was only a young boy. To this day, I love listening to Bro. Roloff's Family Altar program. I thank God that my dad gave my siblings and me great heroes and role models like Lester Roloff, Jack Hyles, John R. Rice, Myron Cedarholm, Curtis Hutson, Harold Sightler, Tom Malone, and many others.

Dad would oftentimes point out some of the world's heroes, and he would comment, "You know, that guy drinks or that guy is not faithful to his wife. He would consistently warn against making the world's heroes our heroes. "Get to the great men," he would say. "Go to the ones who are doing something for God."

I'm so thankful that my dad was careful to teach his children about not idolizing the world's icons. He pointed my siblings and me toward godly people who loved the Lord Jesus Christ, and he would highlight the characteristics that made those people godly. He would make statements like, "It would thrill my heart to know you were a lot like that man right there. He's faithful, loves God, loves his wife, serves the Lord, drives a Sunday school bus, and faithfully brings his family to church."

2.
DO NOT BE TALKED INTO CHANGING YOUR BIBLICAL CONVICTIONS.

M Y FATHER RECEIVED a tremendous amount of pressure from his peers and friends who had kids our age. They would say, "Richard, let your kids do such-and-such." Dad would not allow us to go swimming with people of the opposite gender. He would not allow us go to a movie theater, even though some of our friends had started allowing their teenagers to go. He also insisted on Christlike dress standards. His friends would say, "Richard, lighten up."

He answered, "No, I'm not doing that. I'm not going to change. If the Bible was good then, it's good now. Though the world changes and continues to move to the left, my kids are still going to do right. I already know they will move a little bit left of my stand. I don't want them to move very far, so I will stay a little bit further to the right." He carefully explained his stand with love.

When I was with my friend whose dad wanted to take me to see a movie, my dad firmly but graciously said no. Instead of going to the movie, my friend's dad took us boys to a race-car track where we rode gocarts instead of going to the movie. Today I am very thankful I have never seen what happens on movie screens. I've not seen the nudity I could have seen. I've not heard the profanity I could have heard. I've not seen the suggestive innuendos I could have seen. The Bible says in

Acts 4:20, *"For we cannot but speak the things which we have seen and heard."* What goes in our eyes and ears does affect the heart, our thinking, and our decisions. I am grateful my dad was strong enough to keep that from happening in my life.

My dad would not be talked into changing biblical convictions. Dad possessed more of the nature of a prophet, but I'm more of a servant. My temperament is not to be a fighter; I don't like to fight. So much of my constitution to keep things straight and hold a line has come from my dad. I have watched many of my peers change convictions and standards they once embraced but no longer practice. Places that were once off-limits are no longer off-limits to them. What they once did not tolerate is now permissible.

> Jude 3, 4: *"Beloved, when I gave all diligence to write unto you of the common salvation, it was needful for me to write unto you, and exhort you that ye should earnestly contend for the faith which was once delivered unto the saints. ⁴For there are certain men crept in unawares, who were before of old ordained to this condemnation, ungodly men, turning the grace of our God into lasciviousness, and denying the only Lord God, and our Lord Jesus Christ."*

Wicked men will creep into a person's life, into his home, into his church, into his youth group, and into his school. They come in unawares and deny the only Lord God, our Lord Jesus Christ. These words may seem a bit harsh, but they are cause for parents to be concerned enough to protect their children.

II Timothy 3 talks about perilous times. Verse 14 says, *"But continue thou in the things which thou hast learned and hast been assured of, knowing of whom thou hast learned them."*

What are we to continue in? We are to continue in the things that we have learned and been taught.

The next three verses (Vv. 15-17) all address the precious Word of God. If the Scriptures were right then, they are still right now. *"For I am the* LORD, *I change not..."* (Malachi 3:6). Men change, philosophies change, and methods change, but believers should be just as true as the Bible is true. Stay with the truth! Don't be talked into changing your biblical convictions. Everything we believe has to be birthed out of the Bible. What we believe is converted to principles. Our principles give birth to our convictions, which allow us to put standards of holiness on ourselves so we can be true to the Word of God.

We have to be different to make a difference. The world does not need another cheap imitation of itself. The Christian and the church should be very different than the world. Many spiritual compromises are being made in an effort to reach greater numbers and to satisfy the carnal interests of the lost and saved alike.

Buildings, bodies, and bucks are not indicators of a successful spirituality. If that were the case, then the Las Vegas strip is a successful church. A great church exists when the Lord Jesus Christ is pleased, the Word of God is prioritized, the Spirit of God is comfortable, and the Gospel of God is preached. Don't let someone take away your spiritual convictions. The church does not meet to impress any human being; it's meant to impress the Lord Jesus Christ Who founded the church and is the head of the church. All of the glory is to go to Him. The goal of every Bible-believing church is to exalt the Saviour, to preach the Word, and to show the love of God through its congregants. These goals will remain if the people are not talked into changing their biblical convictions.

Galatians 4:9 says, *"But now, after that ye have known God, or rather are known of God, how turn ye again to the weak and beggarly elements, whereunto ye desire again to be in bondage?"* This verse is saying that once a man has known God and God has known him, and he has even made Him known, why would that man return to the sewer of the world? Why would he go back to drinking alcohol? Why does he go back to looking exactly like the world? Why would he return to the beggarly elements from which God rescued him? Why not stay on the highway of holiness and do right?

That's the question the apostle Paul asked the church of Galatia. After knowing the Spirit of God, the Word of God, and the peace of God, why would anyone go back to the world which has nothing for him?

So many Christians make this choice. I thank God they are still saved, still going to heaven, and still spending eternity with us, but they're not living to please their Father. In John 8:29, Jesus says, *"...I do always those things that please him* [the Father]." When a Christian decides to do what would please God, it is a great day. Ask yourself: what would make God happy? Not what would *appease* Him, but what would *please* Him.

Instead of dedicating ourselves to please God, we ask questions:

- "What's wrong with that?"
- "Why can't we go here?"
- "Why can't we do this?"
- "What is such a big deal about that?"

Do you really want to know what the big deal is? It doesn't please God! If it is doubtful, don't do it. When a Christian stands before God, he will be very glad for anything he has said no to in order to delight the Lord.

Sometimes people say, "I don't want to belong to a church where we always hear, 'No, we can't do this. No, no, no, no...'" You know, it's easy to say no when you have a greater yes. When I love my wife, Linda, it is easy to say no to anything that would grieve her. When I love Christ, it's easy to say no to that which He doesn't love.

Why does God say, *"Love not the world, neither the things that are in the world. If any man love the world, the love of the Father is not in him"?* Only what pleases the Lord should be the Christian's consideration.

I Timothy 4:7, *"But refuse profane and old wives' fables, and exercise thyself rather unto godliness."* Refuse to be caught up in whatever the philosophies, traditions, and cultures of a society are and exercise yourself rather unto godliness. Don't let someone influence you to change your standards. Galatians 5:7 says, *"Ye did run well; who did hinder you..."?* We are more prone to suggestions, blogs, and enticements when we are divided, discouraged, distracted, and depressed.

I wasn't always happy when my dad took a stand that affected me. I cannot begin to express today how very grateful I am that my dad was strong enough to keep my eyes from seeing and my ears from hearing the world's enticements.

3.

DON'T LET YOUR CHILDREN COPY OUTLANDISH HAIRSTYLES OR THE FADS OF THE WORLD.

M Y FATHER WALKED guard on his family and because I was his firstborn, he was especially strict on my hair, dress, and anything that reeked of the world. Oftentimes I didn't understand his rules, but today I am so thankful for his adherence to verses like Romans 12:2, which says, *"And be not conformed to this world: but be ye transformed by the renewing of your mind, that ye may prove what is that good, and acceptable, and perfect, will of God."* He often quoted I John 2:15, which says, *"Love not the world, neither the things that are in the world. If any man love the world, the love of the Father is not in him."*

I think of Titus 2:11, 12, which says, *"For the grace of God that bringeth salvation hath appeared to all men, [12]Teaching us that, denying ungodliness and worldly lusts, we should live soberly, righteously, and godly, in this present world."* This world does not need another cheap imitation of itself. I am saddened when young people try to imitate the world's icons in their hairstyles and in their dress.

My dad watched his children carefully. Occasionally he would say to me, "John, you've been hanging around with so-and-so, haven't you?"

When I would respond, "Nah," in a noncommittal way, he

would reply, "Oh, yes, you have. I can tell by the way you talk, by the way you walk, and by the way you're dressing. Pull up your pants, son."

All the while he was talking, I was thinking, "How could you possibly know?" He made it his business to know because he knew that who I was around was who I would become. I'm thankful for my dad's insistence that I do right.

4.

MAKE SURE YOUR BOYS GET A GOOD HAIRCUT, NOT A PERM OR A STYLE.

I CORINTHIANS 11:14 SAYS, *"Doth not even nature itself teach you, that, if a man have long hair, it is a shame unto him?"* My dad used to sing the following song to my brothers and me:

> *"I Corinthians eleven is still in the Book.*
> *I know that it is 'cause I just took a look.*
> *For a man to have long hair, it says it's a shame,*
> *So why bring disgrace to my dear Saviour's name?"*

My dad wholeheartedly believed in I Corinthians 11:14, and he followed what the Bible taught.

When my dad said, "Go get a haircut, John," that's exactly what I would do. I didn't get it permed or styled; I got it cut. Dad would add, "Don't be an embarrassment to yourself. It's a shame for a man to have long hair." In other words, for a man to have long hair is an embarrassment.

In the Bible, John the Baptist, Samuel, and Samson never had their hair cut, and their long hair was an embarrassment to them. They bore that embarrassment for the sake of the name of God. They had taken a sacred vow. Jesus did not have long hair because He was not a Nazarite. Though He was from Nazareth, he was not a Nazarite.

Artists of the past and the present have depicted Jesus with long hair, but I do not believe that God would put I Corinthians 11 in the Bible and rebel against Himself (the Word) and wear long hair. The fact that coins of that time period depict men with short hair is indicative of how the men wore their hair.

The distinction between the genders is very important to God. Hair length is one way to show this distinction; another way is through attire. We live in a society where the unisex movement has remained very popular. Often the male gender wears long hair, and the females wear short hair. The female gender wears the trousers, and the male gender now wants to wear female attire. How sad!

Dress is important in four primary ways: for protection, for modesty, for a distinction between the genders, and for a testimony. Every Christian needs to evaluate what he or she wears for protection, for modesty, for distinction, and for the testimony of the Lord Jesus Christ.

5.

DO NOT ALLOW ANY ROCK MUSIC, COUNTRY AND WESTERN, OR CONTEMPORARY CHRISTIAN MUSIC.

M Y DAD STRICTLY enforced this particular "proverb." The Bible says in Psalm 25:7, "*Remember not the sins of my youth, nor my transgressions....*" Paul told Timothy, "*Flee also youthful lusts* [youthful desires]..." (2 Timothy 2:22). Many adults struggled with their music standards in their youth, and they continue to justify that struggle, keeping CDs and loading the music on their electronic devices. When that attraction and desire started in their youth, they liked the music so much it became a part of their person. For a person to let go of something he tends to justify can be very difficult.

SOME BIBLICAL PRINCIPLES ABOUT MUSIC

1) **Music is for God.** "*...Make a joyful noise unto the LORD, all ye lands. Serve the LORD with gladness: come before his presence with singing*" (Psalm 100:1, 2). God wants us to sing and participate in the music that He likes. Sometimes people come to church and leave because they don't like the old-fashioned music. Churches need to make sure that God is honored with the music.

When a Christian considers a piece of music, he needs to ask, "Would this music hurt the Lord?" If the music pushes the envelope, he should not really be interested in using it. Some pastors justify their music standards by saying, "You will never have a sizable church because you're too strict on music." Really? Shouldn't we care more about what pleases the Lord? After all, music is for the Lord. May I add here that a church is not measured by its size but by its likeness to Jesus Christ.

2) **Music starts in the heart.** "...*Making melody in your heart to the LORD*" (Ephesians 5:19). Music is a very powerful tool that affects a person's thinking, feelings, and desires.

3) **Music is a medium that teaches.** Most of us learned our ABC's by means of a song. One of the first songs we learn in Sunday school is "Jesus Loves Me." I personally learned many Scripture songs through music. "*Unto thee, O LORD, do I lift up my soul*" (Psalm 25) and "*I will lift up mine eyes unto the hills, from whence cometh my help*" (Psalm 121:1) are examples.

In Ezekiel, the Bible describes how Satan was formed with pipes and music within him. I am not surprised that Satan uses the tool of music to capture the heart of a young person and influence people of all ages. Music is definitely a medium that Satan loves to use. As the former musician of heaven, it is only natural that he would use the wrong kind of music to infiltrate people's lives. Now many have embraced contemporary Christian music—the blending together of the world's music and spiritual words. Almost everywhere we go, we hear music. At the mall, music is blaring out of the stores to draw in shoppers. At Christmastime we're captivated by the music that we heard and learned as children. Music captures our hearts and minds.

My friend, contemporary Christian rock and its cousin rock 'n' roll are very sexual in connotation. This next statement may seem blunt, but I believe Christian rock can be compared to Christian pornography. *Christian* and *rock* do not go together just like *Christian* and *pornography* do not go together! God doesn't borrow from Satan and his realm in order to receive holy worship to Himself or to edify His children!

Psalm 40:3, *"And he hath put a new song in my mouth, even praise unto our God...."* Although God puts a new song in our hearts, an appetite for the right kind of music still has to be developed. Filtering our minds from worldly music is very important.

I had the privilege of leading a man to Christ years ago. He was doing so well, and he was going through discipleship. One Friday night I couldn't get in touch with him. When I couldn't find him on Saturday and then again on Sunday, I knew something was wrong. I found that he had gone on a drug binge, and his relapse was so disheartening. When he came back to the Lord, he told me that he had gotten rid of all his worldly music, but one night after work, he starting thumbing through the music stations until he found a country and Western station. He started listening to song after song, and before he knew it, he headed to the local bar to drink and to hear more. He was soon easily tempted to return to his former wicked crowd.

He said, "Once I had a few drinks, my resistance was shattered. I found some drugs and went on a seven-day journey away from God. I lost my job. Pastor, it all started with one song—the wrong kind of music that weakened my resistance."

Probably my most challenging situation with music involved a sixth grader named Peter I met during my early years of teaching school. He was a good, smart boy whose grades suddenly plummeted. His mother was concerned, and I became so concerned I went over to his house. Peter's mother wasn't a Christian, but he had accepted the Lord. When I visited, I discovered he had been listening to self-destructive music that talked of suicide. I started reading the titles of the songs, and when I told the Peter he needed to get rid of that music, he responded in harsh anger. "No! You're not taking my music!" I was somewhat surprised by his response because Peter had always been a kind boy.

When I tried to explain that the music was hurting his spirit and therefore his grades, and even his mom, he screamed, "I don't care! This is the only thing I have!" He slipped on his headset and continued screaming, "Get out! Get out! I'm not going to listen to anybody!" As a sixth grader, Peter had developed an addiction that had taken him down a wrong road.

Through the years of dealing with those with worldly music addictions, I'm thankful my dad saw fit to watch carefully what my siblings and I listened to. Ephesians 5:18, 19 says, *"And be not drunk with wine, wherein is excess; but be filled with the Spirit. Speaking to yourselves in psalms and hymns and spiritual songs, singing and making melody in your heart to the Lord."* People who get away from God oftentimes begin to entertain the wrong kind of music.

In my opinion, if Christians do not address two particular issues and follow God on them, they will cripple themselves from being the vibrant Christian God wants them to be. One is music, and the second is money. If you are not willing to address how you spend, invest, and make money, you will struggle spiritually. You will not be the Christian you should be. Neither can you live a holy life on a diet of ungodly music or even, in my opinion, contemporary Christian music. The wrong kind of music will definitely hurt you as it numbs your spiritual senses.

Parents have a responsibility to walk guard on their children's music choices. The Devil is extremely wise, and one of his tactics is to get them hooked on what's wrong in their youth. He whets their desires so he will have them the rest of their lives.

CHRISTIAN EDUCATION

*Christian education
doesn't* cost;
it pays.

– Bill Harvey

CHRISTIAN EDUCATION
IS A MUST.

I CERTAINLY UNDERSTAND that not everyone agrees with this particular principle. I attended public school for my first two years of school. In second grade, I was fast conforming to the world's ways. I have already shared the story of not wanting to give a Bible to a classmate for his birthday. That incident happened when I was in the second grade after being invited to go to a classmate's party. Dad purchased a toy for my classmate, and he also got a Bible for him. I was embarrassed by the gift because I knew he wasn't a Christian, and I was a Christian.

I feel relatively sure Dad had a conversation with my mom about my attitude, and they planned to find a way to get me out of that environment, and they did—at no small cost. When I entered the third grade, my parents enrolled all of their school-aged children into a Christian school. Wherever we moved, my parents found a Christian school for us to attend, or we were home educated. Being home-educated lasted for about four months because we nearly drove my mother to the funny farm! My mother was a teacher, but when she tried to teach four teenage boys, the task became overwhelming to her. We were not the best sons at that time. The truth is, we were a heaviness to our mother, so we went back to Christian school. My parents sacrificed dearly to make sure we were in Christian schools. My dad believed firmly that Christian education was the only option.

Christian schools aren't perfect, but my dad was always very attentive to our Christian school setting. He made sure he knew the kids attending that school; he watched how they dressed, how they responded, how they drove, and even what they listened to. He was very in tune to the kids in our schools, and he always watched the friends we chose because no Christian school is without negative influences. In the very best of schools, there is a group of kids to avoid. My dad believed in being nice to everybody but not hanging around with wrong people.

Proverbs 14:7 says, *"Go from the presence of a foolish man, when thou perceivest not in him the lips of knowledge."* Leave the presence of the person who doesn't have the right kind of attitude. Let him stand by himself as he goofs around, tells off-color jokes, or rebels against his family. Let him be foolish alone and by himself; don't join in with him. Psalm 1:1 states, *"Blessed is the man that walketh not in the counsel of the ungodly, nor standeth in the way of sinners, nor sitteth in the seat of the scornful. But his delight is in the law of the* LORD; *and in his law doth he meditate day and night."* How often will you find someone in the public school delighting in the law of the Lord?

While preaching in Missouri one time, I met a lady who said, "I remember when you used to say your verses to me." She had volunteered at the school I attended to listen to the children say the verses they had memorized. I had a daily Bible memory program, and I would quote the verses to her.

To this day, I am so thankful for those who taught me and encouraged me to memorize the Bible. Happy is the child or young person who delights himself in the law of the Lord, who doesn't walk in the counsel of the ungodly, and who doesn't stand in the way of sinners.

Jeremiah 10:2, which is one of my favorite verses, says, *"Thus saith the L*ORD*, Learn not the way of the heathen...."* Be simple toward the things that are evil and wise to things that are good. Knowing the latest gossip in *People* magazine or on *TMZ* will not be Christ-honoring. Learning the way of the heathen is absolutely detrimental to the health of the Christian.

I believe Instagram and Facebook can be very helpful to some extent; unfortunately, I think people often learn about matters they shouldn't learn about because of information that comes through their newsfeed. If it's questionable, stay away from it! We don't have to, nor do we need to address posts that are only meant to grab our attention and whet our curiosity. We should abstain from being curious about the questionable. We should "Glory in not knowing," as Dr. Wendell Evans often quoted.

For many years, Dr. Roy Thompson served as the pastor at Cleveland Baptist Church in Cleveland, Ohio. For many of those years, he was not in favor of Christian education. As a matter of fact, he believed that Christian kids should to be missionaries in the public schools. After years of sending his kids to public school for evangelism purposes, he began losing his kids. I personally heard him say, "After promoting the evangelization of the public school for several years, I feel like I'm wrong, and we need to start a Christian school." He started a Christian school that is still in existence.

He explained his stance by using the following analogy: "For all of these years, I've sent canaries into a cage of sparrows to teach the sparrows to sing. After watching this process over time, I realize all my canaries can now do is chirp. I sent my kids in to evangelize, and unfortunately the sparrows, the unsaved kids, took away their song."

I am for missionaries, but I do not think the average child or teenager is strong enough to be immersed in the public school environment and not be adversely affected. My dad believed parents needed to shelter their children in a place where the Word of God and good principles were taught at any cost.

If you feel you cannot afford the tuition, disconnect your cable television. Repair your old car instead of going into debt for a new vehicle. Make some adjustments in your eating out and then go to your knees in prayer. God loves your children more than you love them and can help you provide for them!

I see Christian education as an investment in the lives of my children. If the Christian school were an absolute impossibility, then I would find a way to educate them at home in a Christian environment. My dad believed this principle wholeheartedly, and I believe he was right.

CONCLUSION

The principle of
affection,
correction,
and direction

Conclusion

As I have considered my father's life, I believe he had three guiding principles, which closely align with a lesson I once heard from a businessman. These three words that best describe my father and my mother also describe other parents who honor the Lord. I lived with a father who was not perfect, but he was sincere. He was what he was. I believe these three guiding principles of my father will be helpful to every parent.

The Principle of Affection

Everybody needs to be loved, but children especially need to be loved. One of the greatest gifts that parents can give their children is affection. Someone has said that approximately 70 percent of parenting is convincing and reminding your children that you love them. Show it, tell it, write it—do whatever it takes for your children to know that you love them. My father was very good at expressing his love in numerous ways. Though Dad was not reared in a loving family, he would say, "I love you, John" every single day.

Three Ways for Parents to Express Love

Tell it because people need to hear they are loved. Kids especially need to hear it. Telling your love is not always saying "I love you." Sometimes it is saying, "Boy, you're really good at that." Or "I love the way you respond when I ask you to do something." Complimenting your child is a great way to demonstrate your love. Learning to speak good words to your children is vital.

The story of Solomon's son Rehoboam is one with tragic consequences. When he became the king of Israel, Rehoboam sought the older men for counsel. For the people to follow him and be his servants forever, they advised Rehoboam to serve the people, to speak good words to them, and to respond to their needs. That advice sounded like work to Rehoboam, so he sought advice from his peers who told him to do exactly the opposite. Because he listened to his friends instead of taking the advice of the older men, he quickly split the kingdom. Rehoboam could have loved his people had he responded to their needs and used good words to sustain his kingdom.

Every child needs love and needs a lot of it. Tell it. Say it. Speak your love. My father would say, "John, you're good at this." (I wouldn't even agree with him half the time.) When he attended my basketball game and I would cross the half-court line with the ball, he would yell, "Shoot it! Shoot it! Put your weight behind it!"

He believed every shot I took was going to go in the basket. I would say, "Dad, please quiet down. I'm not that good of a shot."

"Oh, son, you just don't believe in yourself. You've got to believe in yourself. Shoot it. Shoot it." Dad believed in speaking powerful, encouraging praise. Sometimes parents will get what they praise for—not what they complain or nag about. A parent's words are extremely important. A leader's words are important. Words show love and affection, so tell your love.

Type **or write your love.** Put your love in print. The other day I enjoyed going through some letters that my dad wrote to me while I was in college.

We live in a day where everybody texts and emails, but nothing is wrong with a handwritten note. I'm thankful for the letters I received. Dad always wrote, "I love you," in his letters. When he served in the Army, he was stationed in Germany. While there, he learned to say, "Ich liebe dich," which is "I love you" in German. He would often write "Ich liebe dich" on the back of an envelope. Dad verbalized his love, and he put it in print.

Years ago I had the privilege of baptizing an older man named John who became a very vibrant witness for Christ. When I would ask visitors who came to church how they heard about our church, many would say, "An old man gave me a tract downtown at the bus stop." I was always encouraged when I saw John. He lived alone on the tenth floor in an apartment building in downtown Long Beach. One day he didn't come to church, but he didn't have a phone for me to check on him. When I went to check on him, he didn't respond to my knock on his door.

A couple of days later his nephew unexpectedly called and said, "Pastor Wilkerson, I don't know you, but you've got to be important to my uncle, so I wanted you to know he passed away at his house. When I went to his home, I found a stack of 15 to 20 notes beside his nightstand, and they're all from you. I started reading your notes to my uncle, and I thought, *He doesn't have any notes from me.* I know because of where he kept them that they were very important to him. Would you come over and help me work through his personal affairs? Would you also help me do a service for my uncle?"

My purpose in sharing this illustration is not to pat myself on the back. Rather, I am reminding us that when God told us He loved us, He wrote it down. We also need to write reminders of our love to others.

Do your kids have a note from you that tells them my dad

or my mom loves me? Do your parents have a note from you that says my son or my daughter loves me? Type your love! Write your love!

Show your love by *touch*. Be affectionate. Every child needs touch—holding hands, tousling his hair, putting your arm around her, giving him a light punch on the arm. Children enjoy having affection shown to them. Everybody is different and receives love differently. The love language of some is touch, while another may be less responsive in this way. Because every person is different, learn his or her love language.

Dads, if you are rearing girls, realize they need a dad to hold their hand, put an arm around them, and hug them occasionally. They need him to sit with them and to take them places. Boys need a dad who will put his arm around their shoulder, pull them close, and enjoy the camaraderie created. Let your children know that you love them; they need your affection and love. In Psalm 127:1, 2, the Bible tells us, *"Except the LORD build the house, they labour in vain that build it: except the LORD keep the city, the watchman waketh but in vain. ²It is vain for you to rise up early, to sit up late, to eat the bread of sorrows: for so he giveth his beloved sleep."* The person who is loved feels a great amount of security.

Every wife has a need to be loved, but sad to say, many men are lousy lovers. That's why God has to tell a husband to love his wife. A wife feels love through *talk*, through *type*, and through *touch*.

My dad happened to be a hugger; he tousled our hair, slapped us on the back, and put his arm across our shoulders. I thank God for his affection in my life; I know his touch gave me security. I shared about the time I felt my parents' marriage was in trouble, but when I saw them holding hands, their touch assured me they loved each other. Show affection through what you say and by what you write.

Saying, "I'm not real good at writing" is no excuse for not writing. Write something simple on a sticky note and affix it to a steering wheel. Figure out something you can write that would be meaningful to your child. Learn to speak good words to your children. Speak good words to your spouse. Speak good words to your parents. Words are powerful. *"A word fitly spoken is like apples of gold in pictures of silver"* (Proverbs 25:11). Ephesians 4:29 says, *"Let no corrupt communication proceed out of your mouth, but that which is good to the use of edifying...."* The word *edifying* means "building up." Our words should be good words that build.

The people you love to be around the most are people who speak good words to you. We get excited when some people come into a room; we get excited when certain others leave the room, and usually the issue revolves around that person's mouth. They either breathe words of edification, or they breathe destruction or corruption.

John 17 speaks of the intercessory prayer of Jesus. During the hours in the garden of Gethsemane before His betrayal, God allowed us to know what Jesus prayed. He prayed for you, and He prayed for me. Jesus interceded for those who would believe on Him after He went back to be with the Father. He also prayed for His disciples; He prayed that God would not take them out of the world but that God would keep the world from them.

"Father, I will that they also, whom thou hast given me, be with me where I am; that they may behold my glory, which thou hast given me: for thou lovedst me before the foundation of the world... ²⁶*And I have declared unto*

them thy name, and will declare it: that the love where-
with thou hast loved me may be in them, and I in them"
(John 17:24, 26).

That the Son felt loved by the Father can be easily seen in these
verses. He said to the Father, "You've loved Me from the foundation of the world."

Stable and secure is the young person who knows his parents
and his authorities love him. Satan loves to put walls between
important relationships: father and children, mother and children, husband and wife, pastor and people, boss and employees,
and between friends. Satan is the one responsible for sowing dis-
cord among people. He is the one who's the accuser of the brethren. Be careful about being critical because Satan fuels a critical
nature to keep walls erected between important relationships.
Children benefit from large amounts of affection.

THE PRINCIPLE OF DIRECTION

Every child needs direction. Someone said affection is
probably 70 percent of child rearing. If a child knows he's loved,
he will be secure. Children who feel loved will be open to influence; therefore, they need somebody to provide that direction.
My dad gave me direction, and I have tried to follow in his
footsteps by providing my children with godly direction.

On several occasions, I have had one or more of my children seek my advice. "Dad, I don't know what to do. Would
you direct me about what to do? I know you'll make the best
decision." What they mean is, "I know Dad loves me." When
they are convinced of my love, they will trust me to help them
with their decision making. A child who is loved and wants to
be successful needs someone to give him direction.

In Genesis 18, Abraham is being visited by God's messengers. I believe one of the messengers was an Old Testament appearance of Jesus Christ (a Christophany). The visitors were talking about the destruction of Sodom and Gomorrah when a question arose:

> *"And the men rose up from thence, and looked toward Sodom: and Abraham went with them to bring them on the way. And the LORD said, **Shall I hide from Abraham that thing which I do;** Seeing that Abraham shall surely become a great and mighty nation, and all the nations of the earth shall be blessed in him? For I know him..."* (Vv. 16-19).

What God knew about Abraham is explained in verses 19 and 20.

> *"For I know him, that **he will command his children and his household after him,** and they shall keep the way of the LORD, to do justice and judgment; that the LORD may bring upon Abraham that which he hath spoken of him. And the LORD said, Because the cry of Sodom and Gomorrah is great, and because their sin is very grievous."*

How many children did Abraham have at this time? None! Yet the Bible says that God knew *"...he will command his children...."*

Three Ways for Parents to Direct Their Children

1) **We direct our children through *teaching*.** Deuteronomy 6:6, *"And these words, which I command thee this day, shall be in thine heart...."* According to this Scripture, the first thing God wants me to do is have His Word in my heart. Verse 7 continues, *"And thou shalt teach them diligently unto thy children, and shalt talk of them when thou sittest in thine house, and when thou walkest by the way, and when thou liest down, and*

when thou risest up." God tells parents four times in this passage when they should teach their children. Basically, teaching should be for every child, every available time—all the time.

A parent needs to constantly talk to his children. Perhaps you see a drunk who is stumbling around on the side of the road. You can laugh and point, or you can use it as a teachable moment and address the results of drunkenness. You can ask, "What's wrong there? What do you think the problem is?" When you see someone who is not dressed properly, you can say, "Oh, my!" or you can say, "I wonder what the situation is there? What can we learn from that?" Whenever you evaluate what you see, when you listen to something on the radio, or when you see something questionable on television, you can use that time to talk to and teach your children about Biblical things versus the philosophies of the world.

As we use these times to teach our children, we will even be renewed in our own mind. After all, all of us have unwittingly received a lot of programming in this world system while sitting in front of a television or other media or listening to music. Oftentimes that programming overshadows what we have in the Word of God. The Bible tells us in Isaiah 54:13 that if we get the Word of God into the hearts of our children, the peace of our children will be great.

Sometimes to break my heart, I will park outside of a public school to watch the children leave the buildings at the end of the day. I grieve as I see hopelessness in their eyes—in the way they think, the way they act, and the things they say. Most of them lack peace because they don't have the Word of God. If we want to give our kids direction, we have to teach our children biblical truth.

2) **We direct our children through *training*.** Proverbs

22:6, *"Train up a child in the way he should go: and when he is old, he will not depart from it."* Every child needs the attention of training. I must confess it is easier for me to rake my yard alone than to rake it with my kids. Training my children to work is more difficult than simply doing the job. Training is important, time-intensive, and investment-intensive. Help your children to know how to do certain things in a right way. Training your children is a responsibility in directing them in the way they should go.

3) We direct our children through the use of *tutors*. God uses other people as an extension of parents in the lives of children. If my kids needed my help to do calculus, I couldn't help them. I have not the first concept of how to work those problems! Instead, I would seek the help of a tutor who understood calculus. I'm so glad that God gave us pastors, Christian school teachers, youth workers, Sunday school teachers, camp counselors, and youth conference speakers to help tutor our children.

My father sought help for us from tutors. He once pawned his and Mom's wedding bands so two children could go to camp. My dad saw the wisdom in getting some other servants of God to provide something that they couldn't provide in the confines of their home. I will never forget the preaching service at camp when one of my brothers surrendered to serve the Lord. I remember watching one of my brothers sob, "God, I'll serve You. I'm going to serve You." I remember kneeling and praying near him. That night at camp was monumental in the life of my brother. I had no idea the sacrifice my parents were making to assure that we got on that bus and got to camp.

When I attended Youth Conference in Hammond as a teenager, I don't think my parents had two pennies to rub together at the time. I came for a week, and during the Thursday afternoon service in what is now the Jack Hyles Memorial Auditorium, I surrendered myself to serve the Lord because of the great love and investment of my parents and their training.

THE PRINCIPLE OF CORRECTION

Every child needs correction. In the day and time in which we live, parents need to see the importance of verses on loving discipline. Proverbs 13:24 says, *"He that spareth his rod hateth his son: but he that loveth him chasteneth him betimes."* Every child needs discipline and correction. When they do something wrong, they need somebody to tell them. Instead of jumping all over the teacher, jump all over your child!

Three Ways for Parents to Correct Their Children

1) **Discipline** *correctly.* Coaching kids in sports can be a really wonderful experience; however, far too often the parents create unnecessary problems. Kids are generally fine with the coach's correction, but parents want to throw a fit. Some parents are always taking up for their children at the expense of the blessing of their children. Obviously, children need to be defended on matters that are questionable. However, I think we sometimes defend our children way too much rather than let them take the lumps of life. Let your child bear his yoke in his youth. While they're young and dumb, let them take a few lumps! Allow them to experience loving discipline correctly.

When our son Tyler was a junior in high school, he thought moving the car of one of his buddies would be cute. He and his buddies picked up the back of the car and turned the car sideways in the parking stall. They thought their prank was really funny until they realized they had broken the steering column on the car. Their prank was at the cost of $400.

The father whose car was damaged became obviously upset and shared his frustration with the school principal. As a result of that confrontation, the principal came to my office, told me about the prank, and added that my son was involved.

"Well, let's deal with it. I agree that the boys need to be disciplined. What do you think we should do?"

"I think we should suspend every boy for five days," the principal stated emphatically.

"Five days?" I was shocked by his answer.

"Well, they ought to pay for what they did."

"I agree; they should pay for the damage they caused, but a five-day suspension? Why don't we sleep on it tonight? We'll talk about it tomorrow morning."

He came back the next day and said, "I feel even stronger about the matter. Five days."

"Okay, five days it is." I backed his decision though I thought it was harsh in addition to paying for the damage.

I remember my son's saying, "Dad, five days? Five days of zeroes my junior year? I'm not going to be able to make those grades up."

I hurt for my son, but I said, "You know what, son? Next time you'll learn not to damage someone else's property."

The truth is, I was in disagreement with the principal; I thought his penalty was ridiculous. However, at the time, I did not want my son to know I felt that way. He spent five of the most miserable days of his life at home, working the entire time. "It's not fair," he would say.

"I'll tell you what's not fair, son," I replied. "What isn't fair is for you to move someone's car and cause damage. You will probably keep your hands off of other people's property from now on."

Learn how to help your children go through difficult times that result because they need correction. That means it's the parents' responsibility to correct them. They need someone to guide their thoughts and attitudes. Correct your children consciously. Every parent needs to make that responsible decision and stay on top of it. Many dads nowadays are passive and not active about correcting children. In fact, they are not accountable or responsible in dealing with their children. If mothers have to do most of the disciplining of the children, some issues will arise.

My wife spends more quantity time with our children than I do by virtue of our responsibilities. However, if there are issues in our home, all she has to do is call me. Almost all children (including mine) will hit a wall of rebellion. Some of the most soft-spoken, wonderful kids can be stubborn at times. They will get into a frame of mind, and they think they will win. Parents, you absolutely cannot let them win those little battles! At these times, a father can be very, very important in directing the child's mindset and correcting him. The worst thing a child can do in my home is to give their mom problems. The sternest discipline we've ever had in our home is over showing mom disrespect. I had to make a conscious decision that correction is my responsibility.

2) **Discipline** *calmly.* Correct them calmly, and do not lose your cool. I am embarrassed to admit that I have disciplined in anger. Hopefully the times I have disciplined in anger are the exception, not the rule. Parents, if anger is an issue in your life, you will struggle and likely cause some real problems. Anger will provoke your children to wrath, so keeping your anger under control is very important. To discipline calmly, consider taking a little time before dealing with your child after an event. Some of

their shenanigans will aggravate you and will hurt you. Calm down because losing your temper becomes counterproductive to the process. James 1:20 says, *"The wrath of man worketh not the righteousness of God."* When anger is involved, you generally will not do the right thing. Many an employee who has lost his temper says things he shouldn't say and does things that aren't right. Ephesians 4:31 says, *"Let all bitterness, and wrath, and anger, and clamour, and evil speaking, be put away from you, with all malice."* Don't make excuses as to why you're angry; they will not work.

3) **Discipline** *consistently.* Being consistent in discipline is probably one of the hardest things to do. Knowing exactly what to do when correction is needed takes wisdom and God's guidance. To discipline in love means needing the discernment of the Holy Spirit of God. Parents need the filling of the Holy Spirit of God to know how to help their children. Strive to be consistent.

Every parent needs to incorporate affection, direction, and loving correction in their child rearing. In doing so, I believe they will rear children who are loved by everyone—not just mom and dad.

Thank You

Thank you for allowing me the chance to share these proverbs from my father. I love him and I miss him, but I will forever be thankful for the way he loved and labored to bless my life. I pray that God's wisdom will help each parent to discern the right philosophies and methods by which to rear his children for Him.